D0932607

Though the Fig Tree
Does Not Blossom

Though the Fig Tree Does Not Blossom

Toward A Responsible Theology Of Christian Hope

Ellen Ott Marshall

WIPF & STOCK · Eugene, Oregon

Wipf and Stock Publishers
199 W 8th Ave, Suite 3
Eugene, OR 97401

Though the Fig Tree Does Not Blossom
Toward a Responsible Theology of Christian Hope
By Marshall, Ellen Ott
Copyright©2006 by Marshall, Ellen Ott
ISBN 13: 978-1-4982-3583-9
Publication date 8/27/2015
Previously published by Abingdon Press, 2006

All scripture quotations unless noted otherwise are taken from the *New Revised Standard Version of the Bible*, copyright 1989, Division of Christian Education of the National Council of the Churches of Christ in the United States of America. Used by permission. All rights reserved.

Revised Standard Version of the Bible, copyright 1946, 1952, 1971 by the Division of Christian Education of the National Council of the Churches of Christ in the United States of America. Used by permission. All rights reserved.

For Tommy and Katherine

Contents

Acknowledgments

I have worked on this book in three distinct contexts, each one with its own community of support. At Vanderbilt University, I arrived at my research question while studying with Howard Harrod and Peter Hodgson, both of whom offered encouragement, counsel, and constructive criticism during the book's formative years as a doctoral dissertation. Howard passed away in 2003, but he remains my model for doctoral advising. He was reliable, honest, and kind. Throughout my master's thesis and dissertation, he taught me to faithfully present the views of others through exacting "internal exposition," and he encouraged me to craft my own contribution with equal care. I am also grateful to the other members of my dissertation committee, Victor Anderson, John Lachs, and Bonnie Miller-McLemore.

I had not yet finished the dissertation when I was offered a position as assistant professor at Elizabethtown College in Pennsylvania. There, I was most fortunate to have Christina Bucher as the chair of my department. Chris helped me to limit some of my commitments during the first year so that I could complete the dissertation. But, more than that, she was my friend and mentor, and I will be forever grateful for the patience, insight, and good humor she shared with me. While at Elizabethtown, I also benefited from a workshop and grant through the Wabash Center for

Teaching and Learning in Theology and Religion. This wonderful place gave me invaluable resources for teaching and additional time and support one summer to begin revising the dissertation for publication.

At the Claremont School of Theology, I am indebted to Dean Jack Fitzmier who shepherded me through my first years as a professor in graduate theological education. By expressing confidence in my ability and by buttressing my efforts, Jack provided that miraculous kind of support that only increases one's freedom. I have also been surrounded by wonderful colleagues here, several of whom provided thoughtful comments on this manuscript: Andy Dreitcer, Kathleen Greider, Carol Lakey Hess, and Marjorie Suchocki. During the final stages of revision and manuscript preparation, I relied heavily on Shannon Dunn and Katy Scrogin, who helped me with style and substance and took on even the most tedious task with terrific care and good will. At Abingdon, I have greatly appreciated Bob Ratcliff's enthusiasm for the project.

I am also blessed by a family that journeys through these and all contexts with me. My in-laws, Cynthia and Tom Marshall, embrace me with support that has neither limit nor condition. My parents, Karen and Phil Ott, read this manuscript and applauded its completion just as they have discussed homework at the kitchen table and listened to rehearsals in the dining room all my life. I cherish our continued and growing friendship and am profoundly grateful for the many concrete expressions of their love. My husband, Tommy, has been my companion through each step of this process, from the initial question to the proofs. But the truth is that this book has been one rather intermittent thread running through the fabric of our life together. I am deeply grateful for Tommy's enthusiastic support for this book, but I am more grateful for the larger fabric of our lives and for the many ways Tommy affirms me and attends to my well-being. I must also acknowledge our dog, Beta, since she is the one with whom I most frequently mulled over a question, sorted out a point, played with a phrase, and deliberated the structure of a chapter. These are the things one does while walking the dog! The newest addition to our family is Katherine, who makes herself known in the final chapter of this book. Her presence in our lives gives me joy beyond measure and fills me with gratitude beyond words.

Introduction

ope has a job to do. In the continuous and far-reaching labor
of the moral life, hope is the sense of possibility that generates
and sustains moral agency. Hope's object provides an impetus
for action, a sense of direction, and a cause that renders process meaningful. Hope's sources sustain us along the way. Indeed, hope carries such
obvious import that it seems above reproach. In the Christian tradition,
where we herald it as one of three theological virtues, hope assumes an air
of royalty. In this environment, criticism of hope appears to be a luxury
that real life cannot afford and a prideful expression that faithful life cannot countenance.

However, hope is too important not to engage critically and practice
intentionally. Hope's status as a theological virtue has overshadowed its
everyday employment, such that we treat it like a show horse rather than
a workhorse. It is not enough to be infused with hope by God, as the
Christian tradition teaches. We must also deliberately practice a hope
that is responsible to this world and to the promise and peril that reside
here. In order for hope to perform its function in the moral life, we must
cultivate it in a particular way. If it is to generate and sustain moral
agency, hope must be practiced as ongoing negotiation between the
promising and sobering aspects of life and faith.

This is what I mean by a responsible hope. It is a disposition that remains accountable to promise and peril. It unearths beauty and faces tragedy. It celebrates goodness and knows cruelty. It buoys the spirit and steels the spine. This disposition is not a balanced arrangement of these elements, but rather a dynamic and difficult practice of holding them in tension, of being accountable to the resiliency and the fragility of life. Such practice is a spiritual discipline and an ethical endeavor because it affects character formation and shapes our engagement in the world.

This responsible hope is theological because it orients one toward God's unbounded presence in the world. Because this hope affirms God's presence within every aspect of creation, it enlarges our scope of vision and range of accountability. Therefore, a responsible hope remains accountable to the hopes of others and labors to identify common goods rather than pursuing self-interest. Moreover, a responsible theological hope remains open to wonder and takes joy in mysterious and unreasonable good fortune, but it does not rely on them. In addition to affirming God's unbounded presence in all of creation, responsible theological hope relies on human ability to discern this loving presence and respond appropriately to it. A responsible hope takes root in a relational concept of power, insisting that human effort is required to realize the possible. This is not a hope that relinquishes agency to the unidirectional control of an omnipotent God. Rather, this hope is born when we feel empowered to act.

And yet responsible hope also grapples with powerlessness. This is not a disposition that always embodies the "can-do spirit," though it might at times. More often than not, this is a disposition of "relentless persistence."[1] It involves an honest examination of the world and a complete audit of its life-giving and death-dealing potential. Through this audit, responsible hope identifies possibilities that range from a radical, positive change to the survival of disappointment. And these possibilities—the objects of hope—require constant evaluation and occasional adjustment in light of new information about their viability, connection to a larger good, and implications for others. Sometimes, one practices this hope with the tireless energy of a committed community organizer who is clear about purpose and process. At other times, one practices responsible hope by mourning loss, raging against limitation, and cataloging threats. And in the most desperate times, we may practice responsible hope by forcing ourselves to feel the weight of a friend's hand on our back.

With this recommendation for a responsible hope, I join a diverse conversation. I discuss Aristotle and Aquinas to determine points of compatibility and departure with classical understandings of hope as a virtue. I engage liberation theologians who insist that the object of hope must direct our attention and care toward this creation. I draw from feminist and process thinkers who insist on a relational concept of power. I listen to critics who argue that constructive theological ethics makes an instrumental use of religion, and to skeptics who insist that any language of hope simply clings to the promise of a happy ending in order to silence the elemental questions raised by tragedy. And I converse with friends and strangers who have struggled with hope.

The first chapter presents the problem of hope that this book seeks to address, namely how to cultivate a sense of possibility without glossing over the real losses and limits of life. The second chapter reviews the teachings of Aristotle and Aquinas in order to document points of alignment and departure between this tradition and my constructive proposal. The first main departure is an orientation toward the object of hope that involves a broadened scope of vision rather than a redirected gaze. I join contemporary liberationist theologians who insist that the object of hope must not turn us away from this world, but broaden our concern and vision for it. The second point of departure pertains to concepts of divine power as a source for hope. Here, I depart from the tradition to join process and feminist theologians who understand God's power to be relational in nature. With a relational concept of power, one cannot hope in God without hoping in humanity. The third chapter presents these contemporary theological influences, and the fourth chapter explains my understanding of the object and source of hope more fully. The fifth chapter describes a number of practices of hope, forms of ongoing negotiation between promise and peril.

One thing that I learned as a young person participating in sports and playing music is to practice something in pieces. Yes, sometimes we would scrimmage to prepare for a game, and sometimes we would play a song through in its entirety. But the real work, the real preparation, occurred through countless drills to learn fundamentals and through endless repetition of a few measures of music to learn fingering, tone, and rhythm. It is important to see "responsible hope as ongoing negotiation between promise and peril" as the game or song in its entirety. We work toward this by practicing it in pieces. We commit ourselves to small, difficult exercises that help us to reflect intentionally on experience, evaluate objects of hope, search out hidden sources of hope, and remain accountable to loss. We have to practice responsible hope in pieces because in our most desperate moments, we do not have the physical security, mental and emotional health, and time to reflect intentionally on the disposition of hope as a whole and to foster it purposefully.

My own most desperate moments involved miscarriages, and I begin chapter five with a reflection on my response to the loss, fear, and comfort that I experienced in those months. The practices that I developed at that time are now part of my disposition, part of a larger set of habits that I try to maintain in these happier days with a healthy child. In happier days, a sense of possibility comes more easily. But if my hope is to be a responsible one, I still have work to do. I must engage practices that keep me accountable to life's vulnerability so that my hope does not slip into optimism. If hope is to generate and sustain moral agency, it must forever be cognizant of the obstacles and threats to its object. In places and times of security and health, we must work harder to remain connected to these perils and to those people who struggle under their weight. It is also true that positions of security and health make us more susceptible to despair because we can afford the luxury of choosing to give up. In our desperate moments, a sense of possibility may be hard to come by, but it may also be all we have. In times of comfort, therefore, it is imperative that we "call into presence" those who continue to suffer, grieve, rage, resist, and survive. [2] They keep us accountable to the vulnerability of life *and* to the imperative of hope. If we fall to optimism, we trivialize their suffering. If we fall to despair, we disrespect their memory.

I practice hope with two paintings in mind, *The Charnel House* and *First Steps*, both by Pablo Picasso. I first saw them in 1999 at an exhibit of Picasso's wartime paintings (1937-1945), and they have been my constant companions while writing this book. [3] *The Charnel House* confronts us with chaotic and gruesome images of death. Among the mangled body parts, three faces are unavoidable. One stares directly at us. The other two, with eyes closed and mouths agape, belong to a woman and a baby. In many ways, *The Charnel House* resembles Picasso's *Guernica*. But in that more familiar painting, Picasso extends a lamp into the destruction accompanied by a living face to bear witness to the crime. In *The Charnel House*, the light is replaced with appendages, thrust upward but bound with rope. Each time that I look at this painting, a knot forms in my stomach, my shoulders tighten, and my fists clench. *The Charnel House* absorbs every photograph of pain, every news account of violence, and

Picasso, Pablo (1881-1973) © ARS, NY The Charnel House. 1944-45; dated 1945. Oil and charcoal on canvas, 6' 6 5/8" x 8' 2 1/2". Art Resource, NY

Digital Image © 2002 MoMA, N.Y.

every narrative of human cruelty I know and assaults me with them all at once. It leaves me feeling utterly defeated.

Turning to the other painting feels like coming up for air. *First Steps* is a tender image of a mother supporting her child who is learning to walk. These bodies are stable and strong. The mother's posture is attentive yet serene. And Picasso's cubist style somehow captures the baby's awkward innocence beautifully. This painting enables me to relive this moment with my own daughter. I feel her fingers gripping mine and her weight shifting around. I hear the thud she makes when she falls and the old-lady groans that mysteriously come from her as she rights herself again. In addition to recalling this personal memory, *First Steps* breathes in every photograph of beauty, every news account of kindness, and every narrative of human goodness that I know and embraces me with them. I feel comforted and encouraged.   At times, I orient my whole body toward *First Steps* in order to keep this feeling alive. As soon as I do this, though, I feel

Picasso, Pablo (1881-1973) © ARS, NY First steps, 1943. Yale University Art Gallery, New Haven, Connecticut, U.S.A. Photo Credit : Scala / Art Resource, NY

convicted by the sense that *The Charnel House* is the only place where responsible people should direct their attention. And I turn from the respite of *First Steps* back to the work of *The Charnel House*. Of course, neither orientation is sufficient. What we need—what the moral life requires—is a broadened vision, not a redirected gaze. The disposition of hope that I commend involves looking back and forth between these two paintings. One painting prompts us to grieve, shout, and resist the limitations and losses of life. The other reminds us of the possibilities for growth, love, and freedom residing in the here and now. If we can learn to hold these images in tension, therefore, we may be able to speak about hope without glossing over tragedy or downplaying obstacles. And in this ongoing work of negotiation, we may be able to cultivate a hope that is properly accountable to things experienced and things envisioned, to the vulnerability and fecundity of life, to peril and to promise.

CHAPTER ONE

The Problem of Hope

W hen I look at *The Charnel House*, I hear the Hebrew prophet Habakkuk: "O LORD, how long shall I cry for help, and you will not listen? Or cry to you 'Violence!' and you will not save? Why do you make me see wrongdoing and look at trouble?"[1] Historically, Habakkuk bore witness to the establishment of the Chaldean (Babylonian) empire in Judah in the late seventh century B.C.E.[2] But the language of this book transcends its original context to capture the agony of all people under threat. The Chaldeans "seize habitations not their own" and "gather captives like sand."[3] They "come for violence" and "terror ... goes before them."[4] They scoff at kings and "laugh at every fortress."[5] In the midst of this horror, Habakkuk questions God: "Why dost thou look on faithless men, and art silent when the wicked swallows up the man more righteous than he?"[6]

Having raised his cry, Habakkuk takes his stand at the tower to await the Lord's response. He then writes the vision down as a series of warnings to the Chaldeans. Through five taunts, Habakkuk promises that their crimes will be punished in kind. The references to violence in this brief book are quite overwhelming, as Judith Sanderson notes. "In its three short chapters Habakkuk contains the word 'violence' six times (1:2, 3, 9; 2:8, 17a, b), which is 10 percent of all the occurrences in the Bible. More than that," Sanderson continues, "almost every verse gives a picture of violence even when the word is not used." [7] Indeed, Habakkuk's vision is bloodier than the actual experience because he uses warrior-king imagery to describe God's response. "Thou didst strip the sheath from thy bow, and put the arrows to the string.... Thou didst bestride the earth in fury, thou didst trample the nations in anger.... Thou didst crush the head of the wicked, laying him bare from thigh to neck." [8] All of this God does "for the salvation of thy people." [9]

Having received this vision, Habakkuk waits with tremendous anxiety for it to be realized. "I hear, and I tremble within; my lips quiver at the sound. Rottenness enters into my bones and my steps tremble beneath me. I wait quietly for the day of calamity to come upon the people who attack us." [10] Following this expression of fearful waiting, we find the oft-quoted statement of faith:

> Though the fig tree does not blossom, and no fruit is on the vines; though the produce of the olive fails, and the fields yield no food; though the flock is cut off from the fold, and there is no herd in the stalls, yet I will rejoice in the LORD; I will exult in the God of my salvation. God, the Lord, is my strength; he makes my feet like the feet of a deer, and makes me tread upon the heights. [11]

The book concludes with a protagonist who is reassured. The shouts of chapter one and the taunts of chapter two are replaced here with a quiet yet resolute declaration of faith. These closing verses demonstrate an absolute trust in God as Habakkuk reaches beyond his present situation, replete with causes for despair, to find a source of sustenance, a cause for hope.

This third chapter differs dramatically in form from the previous two, which in turn vary from one another. Indeed, Sanderson notes that these three "very different genres" indicate "different occasions of writing if not different authors." In fact, it is likely that the original book ended with woe (2:20) rather than a psalm (chapter three).[12] It is certainly the case that one often hears the closing declaration of faith without reference to the horror and warning that precede it. However, the biblical and ethical costs of such segmentation are substantial. We may have three different genres, three different occasions of writing, and maybe even three different authors, but the book of Habakkuk presents us with one story, one narrative capturing the heights and depths of human experience. Thus, we lose its ethical import if we disconnect the end from its beginning.

Ethically, divorcing the psalm from rage and woe presents us with a troubling disposition. Indeed, the very element that makes this closing image so inspirational, the stark contrast between experience and faith, also makes it suspect. Is this a disposition that we should adopt amidst the violence of our day? Should we rejoice in the Lord while famine and AIDS ravage southern Africa? Should we "exult in the God of my salvation" while Latino/a immigrants die in the deserts of the southwestern United States?[13] Should we rejoice in the Lord while families mourn loved ones lost in the continuing cycle of violence in the Middle East? Should we "exult in the God of my salvation" while the death toll climbs in the wake of natural disaster? Our world is marked by intractable human conflicts, global displacement, abject poverty, unfathomable cruelty, unrelenting grief, new and persistent illnesses, immovable despots, and environmental devastation. In such a world, Habakkuk's expression of faith next to the barren fig tree rightly gives us pause.

Divorced from the earlier outrage and lament, the closing verses dampen moral agency because they seem to counsel passivity in the face of injustice. Do we really want to commend those who suffer hunger and violence to stand by the barren fig tree? Reading this proclamation of faith through the lens of Christian eschatology raises another concern, namely, that we are invited to turn away from the sobering aspects of life and find hope in a new creation beyond or above this one. It certainly matters who preaches these words, to whom, and in what context. But with the right configuration—or the wrong one, as the case may be— such language may well trivialize the enduring pain of loss and real impediments to freedom and peace. Indeed, to paraphrase another Hebrew prophet, such a response treats the wounds of people lightly. [14]

The closing verses of Habakkuk may well offer an inspirational statement of faith, but they do not suffice as a text of hope. The text of hope must include the opening shout, "How long shall I cry violence and thou wilt not save? Why dost thou make me see wrongs and look upon trouble?" This shout is properly responsive to the world we know. It recognizes grief and gives space to the rupture of tragedy. Held together, this opening shout and the closing resolve comprise a text of hope because they illustrate the work that hope requires, responding to violence and determining to stand fast in its wake.

Moreover, the work of responsible hope also involves grappling with Habakkuk's taunts. That is, if our hope is a responsible one, we must be ever cognizant of its implications for those we consider enemy, other, or in the way. The middle section of Habakkuk shows us the shadow side of hope,[15] and, much as we want to, we must not gloss over it. Rather, we must constantly reevaluate our own hopes in light of the interests of others. The work of hope involves an authentic expression of our deepest desires, an honest examination of their implications for others, ongoing evaluation of partial interests in light of the common good, and critical assessment of the sacrifices of some for the benefit of others.

Taken in its entirety, Habakkuk is a meaningful text on hope, though not necessarily a hopeful text. Habakkuk's story and our interactions with it demonstrate some of the challenges of hope. How do we maintain hope in this dreadful world? How do we express hope without taunt? How do we rejoice in moments of comfort and remain involved in the events that discourage? It should be clear by now that I am not questioning whether to hope. Hope is an absolutely essential element of daily life. We do not live without it. Hope is also a central component of the moral life, whether we understand it as a virtue in classical moral thought or as a critical and prophetic tool, as in contemporary liberation theologies. And, as Jürgen Moltmann pointed out forty years ago, hope is a core element of a faith tradition that "lives from the raising of the crucified Christ."[16] My question is not whether to hope, but how to do so responsibly.

Hope and Moral Agency

In order to explore responsible hope more fully, we need a clearer description of the role that hope is intended to play in the moral life, its "job description." The familiar definition of hope as "a sense of the possible" remains a helpful starting point.[17] From here, we can clearly see the connections between hope, imagination, and agency. In his 1965 text, *Images of Hope*, William F. Lynch, S.J., suggests that hope imagines "what is not yet seen, or a way out of difficulty, or a wider perspective for life and thought."[18] Through the imagination, one transcends the confines of a moment or circumstance. In doing so, one does not deny the circumstance (as Lynch quite rightly points out), but rather places it in the context of other events and experiences. In other words, my awareness of possibilities does not make me oblivious to my current situation. I see this particular

5

circumstance or moment as one among many, and am thus freed from the "prison of the instant," to borrow another phrase from Lynch. [19]

Such an awareness of possibilities gives us momentum. In this sense, hope is fundamentally stimulating. It draws from the imagination, which broadens our sense of possibility, and it provides an impetus for action. At the very least, one challenges his or her situation by refusing to absolutize it. One cultivates the terrifically revolutionary notion that the way things are is not the way they must be. Hope unsettles. It sets us to waiting and to active preparation. Hope "causes not rest but unrest, not patience but impatience. It does not calm the quiet heart, but is itself this unquiet heart in [humankind]," as Moltmann writes. [20]

With similar intent, Paul Tillich described hope as "the tension of our life toward the future." [21] Tillich's use of the word "tension" is important because the sense of possibility is not accompanied by a guarantee that one will glide toward its realization. This marks a crucial distinction between hope and optimism. The Irish Catholic theologian Dermot Lane asserts that hope "struggles with the ambiguity of existence" in a way that optimism does not. "Optimism," Lane continues, "neglects the realities of pain and suffering and evil, especially the vulnerability of the human enterprise." [22] Hope is a sense that something is possible without the presumption that it is assured.

The Virtue of Hope

This line between possibility and assurance is a fine one, however. Indeed, much of the skepticism about hopeful rhetoric comes from recognition that hope easily slips toward optimism, especially when faith claims grease the slide. Indeed, part of Saint Thomas Aquinas's rationale for casting hope as a theological virtue was to increase our sense of possibility.

He, too, perceived the connection between hope and agency. Following Aristotle, Aquinas taught that a virtue is a habit that disposes one to act well, in accordance with a suitable end. And yet, Aquinas also recognized that the intention to act according to a particular end depends, in large part, on whether an individual deems that end to be possible. Left to natural inclinations, he reasoned, human beings may perceive many things to be impossible. However, the theological virtues extend the range of possibility by disposing us to "apprehend by faith what we hope for and love."[23] In sum, the virtue of hope disposes one to see "that [suitable] end as something possible to attain."[24]

The end toward which theological virtues orient us is the final aim, that which is desired for its own sake and not as a means to something else. In the Christian tradition, this highest good is the *basileia tou theou*.[25] The *basileia* is the ultimate object of hope for the Christian, and it is certainly something to be apprehended by faith rather than by "natural" faculties. To describe the *basileia* vision as a faith claim (as I do throughout this book) is to suggest several things. First, and most obviously, one cannot engage in a discussion of the *basileia* vision without admitting a certain degree of agnosticism. We cannot know anything for certain about the *basileia tou theou*. Those who place authority in the Christian scriptures begin with the descriptions offered there and interpret them as their tradition and conscience commend. Scriptural references to the *basileia* vary tremendously and thus spawn an even greater array of interpretations. To describe the *basileia* as a faith claim is, therefore, to acknowledge that it has neither evidence nor consistency to recommend it. Rather, as a faith claim, the *basileia* vision can only be interpreted through scriptural references and described with models and metaphors.

The second point to be made, though, is that multiple interpretations and metaphorical descriptions in no way dampen the meaning of this image. As

The Kingdom of God

the ultimate object of hope for Christians, the *basileia* vision conveys a promise and issues a call. And because this promise and this call are religious in nature, they are binding. That is, as a matter of faith one commits himself or herself to this vision and the hope and responsibilities that accompany it. [26] The many interpretations of the *basileia* ensure a variety of ethical proposals and dispositional effects. In the history of Christian ethics, the reign of God has been used to engender a revolutionary spirit and to quiet revolt, to convey assurance of pardon and to issue a warning of judgment, to describe a vision of what the world can be and to show what it is not, to generate hope for this world and to locate hope in another, new creation. Some of these proposals will be discussed more critically in later chapters. At this point, it is important simply to take note of the binding nature of the faith claim, however it is interpreted. In short, multiple interpretations do not indicate whimsical believers. Rather, the ongoing effort to relate this image to one's particular experience in the world speaks to the believer's determination to keep the faith claim alive, relevant, and meaningful.

The *basileia* vision is not only continuously interpreted in light of historical developments and personal experiences. It also serves as a lens through which believers interpret these events. In Julian Hartt's language, the *basileia tou theou* is a "construing belief." [27] Thus, for example, one interprets particular historical events as anticipating the coming kingdom or glimpses of the *basileia* vision. This aspect of the faith claim is exercised frequently in conversations about hope. Because the Christian tradition teaches that the *basileia* is both now and not yet, it can serve as a source of hope as well as its object. The anticipatory events and the glimpses that one discerns, therefore, function as sources of hope in the present. If, for example, I interpret the *basileia* as a community of peace and justice, then I will interpret the resolution of a conflict as a glimpse of that vision, as a source of hope. Or, to put it in more theological language, such an event may affirm my belief in "God as one who provides possibilities in human life."[28] In either case, I construe a source of hope through the lens of this faith claim.

Contemporary Concerns

This project is prompted not by such affirming experiences, but rather by those moments and events that call this faith claim into question and render language about hope problematic or even suspect. Pointing to the promise of a glorious future glosses over tragedy, downplays suffering, and stifles cries for justice. Similarly, commending the virtue of hope trivializes the enduring pain of loss and real impediments to freedom and peace. The violence, displacement, disparity, degradation, disease, and oppression that mark our world demand steps toward conflict transformation and reconciliation, guarantees of protection and freedom from persecution, social change and economic restructuring, sustainable ecological practices, scientific research and affordable health care, active opposition to authoritarian regimes, and movements to create space for freedom. The depth of destruction and sadness caused by these historical conditions should give pause to anyone who speaks of hope today. And the concrete steps necessary to address these problems should serve as a corrective to abstract references to the *basileia* vision.

In addition to the challenges posed by lived experience, there are also myriad critiques of *basileia* rhetoric from within theological literature. For example, many in the field of theological ethics contest a sense of evolutionary optimism that supports notions of the *basileia* as the end point toward which we are moving. Similarly, there is growing intolerance with imperialist views that set the Christian interpretation of God's reign as the culmination of history or stress exclusionary aspects of eschatological language in the Christian scriptures. Ecofeminists challenge interpretations of the reign of

God that devalue bodies and the earth by promising a new creation beyond or above this one. A model of the *basileia* as somehow beyond or above history is also at odds with the shift toward talk of God as immanent and related to creation. And finally, in exchanges between religion and the sciences, the requisite of plausibility surfaces. Some contemporary theologians, such as James Gustafson, whose work will be discussed later, insist that theological proposals be consonant with scientific understanding.

In light of these theological and historical concerns, contemporary Christian ethics is filled with constructive proposals for the relationship between ideal and real, *basileia* and history. In working with this material, I have found a triadic framework utilized by Ernst Troeltsch and H. Richard Niebuhr to be particularly helpful. Both of these figures studied Christian ethics by examining the relationship between faith claims and historical developments, thus establishing faith, history, and ethics as three interacting elements of a triad. In his mammoth study, *The Social Teaching of the Christian Churches*, Troeltsch expounded his overarching theme that the tradition develops as believers negotiate between the ideals of faith and the realities of history. Moreover, he asserted that Christian ethics is made possible by this practice of negotiation. [29] Thus, *Kompromiss* becomes prescription as well as description. H. Richard Niebuhr utilized Troeltsch's triadic approach in his sociological studies of religion, particularly *Christ and Culture* and *The Kingdom of God in America*. [30]

Drawing on Troeltsch and Niebuhr, I begin with the assertion that the question of hope is really the question of the relationship between faith and history. The extent and content of one's hope are informed by the way in which one understands the relationship between faith and history. Is the *basileia* a historical possibility or not? Does God enter into history, and if so, in what way and to what end? Do the hard sayings represent unattainable ideals or uncompromising expectations for human behavior?

What can we hope for history, for creation, for one another? And where should we root our hope if it is to be sustaining? These are questions about faith and history. Chapter two explores the ways in which some twentieth-century Christian ethicists have responded to them.

It is immediately apparent, however, that these theologians rarely respond to the questions directly without first articulating a concern about the ways other people have responded. A critical move always precedes the constructive one. Their criticisms highlight errors in the arrangement between faith, history, and ethics. For introductory purposes, I have organized this material into two groups. The first includes critiques of hope based on a faith that is seemingly divorced from historical concerns, and the second challenges objects of hope that appear to be restricted to such concerns. The former questions hopes that are unaccountable to history, while the latter takes issue with hopes molded by history.

Theologians in the first category assert that the language of hope must be accountable to history and lived experiences. They insist that faith claims and the hope they engender must direct care and energy toward this creation. Thus, they reject faith claims that locate the object of hope wholly beyond this world, diverting one's attention from it. As a corrective, these theologians interpret the *basileia* vision in light of political and ecological concerns and describe it as a community of peace and justice—or a flourishing planet. Moreover, these constructive proposals construe the *basileia* as historically or organically related to this time and place. Each historical act of justice approximates the kingdom of God. The beauty of the earth alerts us to God's project. [31]

The second category of figures, however, takes issue with such alignment between interpretations of the ultimate object of hope and particular historical or ecological interests. Such a correspondence, they argue, betrays the tendency to construe divine activity according to human interests. One's hope must be tempered by awareness of the way "things really and ultimately are," to borrow a phrase from James Gustafson, whose work represents this cluster of thought. [32] Some scholars in this group are primarily concerned about human pride and scientific plausibility, and are determined to temper excessive aspirations accordingly. Others are skeptical of the Christian tendency to accelerate the move toward assurances in times of tragedy. They recommend giving space to the elemental questions raised in such moments rather than sweeping them under a promising vision of the future.

The people representing these clusters do not generally refer to their work as negotiating the triad of faith, history, and ethics. However, it seems clear to me that each of them examines the relationship between a faith claim and lived experience, finds it to be somehow out of kilter, and offers a correction. All the while, she or he works with an eye toward the consequent effect. On the one hand, faith claims divorced from history produce supernaturalism, asceticism, otherworldly hopes, and apathy toward the needs of community and creation. On the other hand, faith claims molded according to historical interests engender utopianism and false hopes, and thus trivialize the real losses and limits of life. [33]

These arguments reflect the truly complex nature of the triad in which each element affects the others. Such complexity does not worsen the problematic, but rather suggests a way of addressing it. These theologians perceive an imbalance between faith and history that renders a troublesome effect. That is, they take issue with a particular positioning of the three elements. If we simply arrange the balance differently, we will likely err in another direction. The better approach to problems of faith, history, and ethics is to emphasize the dynamism of the triad. To focus my point further, hope should not be understood as one set configuration of faith and history. Rather, we must understand the disposition as a continuous negotiation between faith and history.

In other words, the triadic framework provides not only a method for examining other proposals for Christian hope but also for constructing my own. Hope occupies the space of ethics and must negotiate constantly between faith and history. A responsible Christian hope must remain accountable to a faith tradition with resurrection as its primary symbol and to the world around us with its myriad crucifixions. Moreover, because we find encouragement and trouble in both faith and history, we must push toward an even more dynamic understanding. We must negotiate between—and remain attentive to—promise and peril in both faith and history. All too often, we fail to achieve the necessary balance. We adopt an otherworldly gaze that buoys the spirit by turning away from the sobering realities of lived experience. Or, especially in the academy, we adopt a hypercritical gaze that deconstructs anything unseen in order to be truthful to the way things really are. Neither the otherworldly gaze nor the knowing scowl will do. We need a mediating disposition, one that holds in tandem the promising and sobering aspects of life and faith. We need to cultivate a sense of the possible without glossing over the real losses and limits of life. This is what I mean by a responsible hope.

Conclusion

With these commitments, let us return to the book of Habakkuk. In his vision, Habakkuk receives no assurance that he will live to see these wrongs righted, and this final passage confirms that. Habakkuk's joy does not stem from the assurance that his hopes will be realized in his lifetime. Indeed, the power of the closing verses comes from the stark contrast between experience and emotion. In a land void of possibility, the prophet expresses a sense of hope. His fortitude and faithfulness are inspiring, and his declaration to stand fast functions like Picasso's painting, *First Steps*, reviving us after the trauma of *The Charnel House*. It seems entirely appropriate to hold the final statement of faith, along with *First Steps*, as the texts of hope.

And yet, a responsible hope requires that we grapple with these stories in their entirety. If the final expression of faith and reassurance is divorced or even distanced from the opening lament, then the possibility of an irresponsible or unaccountable hope certainly arises. But what if, upon reading the statement of faith, we return to the opening experience of anguish? I believe that such a return serves us well, a return to Habakkuk's opening lament and to the experiences and events of our day that elicit a similar anguish. We practice responsible hope by reading the story cyclically. We reiterate the shout, we grapple with the taunts, we breathe in the comfort, and we begin again. Just as we must keep both *The Charnel House* and *First Steps* in view, so must we keep the three parts of Habakkuk's story in earshot. In order for Christian ethics to commend hope without glossing over the losses and limits of life, we must learn to look upon trouble and write the vision down, and then look upon trouble once more.

CHAPTER TWO

A History
of Hope

The purpose of this chapter is to examine classical understandings of hope as a theological virtue by drawing most heavily on Saint Thomas Aquinas and his main philosophical influence, Aristotle. Understanding hope as ongoing negotiation between the promising and sobering aspects of lived experience is compatible with the concept of moral virtue described by both Aristotle and Aquinas. Moral virtues are cultivated through doing, and they observe a mean. However, my emphasis on practice and on negotiation distinguishes responsible hope from Aquinas's categorization of hope as a theological virtue since theological virtues are infused in us by God and do not observe the mean. Because I argue that my concept of hope is indeed theological, I must mark and justify these points of departure from Aquinas more exactly.

Saint Thomas Aquinas on Hope

Born into a wealthy family in 1224/5, Thomas Aquinas decided to join the mendicant Dominican Order in 1244. According to Jan Aertsen,

"The Dominicans were the first religious order to make devotion to study one of its main objectives."[1] Following the orders of his superiors, Aquinas completed his own theological studies at the University of Paris, where he later returned to teach. As a professor there, Aquinas wrote the *Summa Theologiae*, from which most of the following material comes. The *Summa* is Aquinas's magnum opus, a multivolume systematic theology that has three main divisions, the first one focusing on God and the third on Christ. The second one focuses on human beings and has an additional subdivision. The first part of the second part (*prima secundae*) treats human beings (their nature, acts, and virtues) in general, while the *secunda secundae* treats them in detail. The writings (dating from 1259 to 1269) follow a common scholastic pedagogy, *disputatio*, involving a series of objections and then refutations in order to argue a single question.[2] For each question, therefore, there are several articles corresponding to different aspects of the question. This style issues in a remarkably detailed analysis, and I will try to represent that detail faithfully without delving too much into concerns that are beyond the scope of this book. I will also interrupt this account of his position in a few places in order to keep track of the exact points of consonance and dissonance with my own proposal. Aquinas's teachings on hope are found in the second part of the *Summa*. He includes a general treatment of this virtue in the *Treatise on the Virtues* (questions 49–67 in the *prima secundae*). Aquinas also discusses hope earlier with question 40, on "Hope and Despair," and later in the *secunda secundae* with questions 17–22 on "Hope."

Aquinas's first extended discussion of hope, then, occurs in the *prima secundae* of the *Summa*, question 40, "Hope and Despair." Here, he describes hope as a contending (rather than impulse) emotion, an appetite that moves toward things rather than an act of cognition, and a help rather than a hindrance to action. He also identifies despair as the contrary of hope, experience as a cause of hope, and hope as a cause of love. And he assures readers that hope abounds in brute animals, the young, and the inebriated! For my purposes, the most helpful teachings in this article are the four characteristics of the object of hope, the description of hope as an appetite rather than an act of cognition, and the discussion of experience as a cause of hope.

The first characteristic of hope is that one hopes only for some good. This characteristic distinguishes hope from fear, which anticipates an evil. Hope anticipates a perceived good. In this first article, Aquinas does not distinguish between subjective and objective goods. Later, however, he describes the object of hope as agreeable, implying subjectivity.[3] Secondly, one hopes for something in the future. This characteristic distinguishes hope from joy, "which regards a present good" that is "already possessed."[4] Thirdly, the object of hope is "arduous and difficult to obtain." Unlike desire, "we do not speak of any one hoping for trifles, which are in one's power to have at any time." This is why Aquinas categorizes hope as a contending emotion. Hope involves things for which we must contend, not trifles that come easily. Fourth, the object of hope is attainable. This characteristic distinguishes hope from despair. Though the object is in the future and the path toward it is arduous, the object is attainable.[5] In sum, "the object of hope is a future good, difficult but possible to obtain."[6]

Aquinas also describes hope as an act of appetite rather than cognition. He teaches that "the activity of the cognitive power is accomplished not by the movement of the knower toward things, but rather according as the things are known in the knower."[7] Cognition involves knowledge of something, whereas the appetite involves movement toward something. Hope is an act of movement, not just knowledge. Therefore, "hope is a movement of the appetitive power ensuing from the apprehension of a future good, difficult but possible to obtain."[8] Cognition may lead to appetite in that one has knowledge of an agreeable object. But hope is more than knowledge because it involves movement *toward* that object.

Aquinas also argues that hope is affected by experience, because experience can be a cause of hope as well as a cause of the failure of hope.[9] He identifies two ways in which something can cause hope, "either because it makes something possible [for] a man or because it makes him think something [is] possible."[10] Experience causes hope in the first sense when a person "acquires the faculty of doing something easily."[11] Here Aquinas references Aristotle's example that success over one's adversaries gives him confidence in future victory.[12] Such an experience increases one's ability and one's expectations of success. Thus, the second way in which experience affects hope is that it makes one "reckon something possible." Aquinas does, however, note that experience can affect hope negatively. Experience "makes a man think possible what he has previously thought impossible; so, conversely, experience makes a man consider as impossible that which hitherto he had thought possible."[13] However, he concludes that experience is a cause of hope, because it affects hope positively in two ways and negatively in only one way.

From this initial discussion, we find hope to be an act of the appetite, insofar as it generates movement toward something. The object of hope is agreeable, future, difficult, and attainable. Hope is caused by things that either make an object possible or make a person think that object is possible to attain. And experience is one such thing.

My understanding of hope is not too far from this initial description. Like Aquinas, I understand hope to be a "contending emotion," an appetite that compels us to move toward an object. I have assumed what Aquinas makes explicit, that one hopes for some good or for something perceived to be agreeable.[14] And I believe that hope moves us forward because we have a sense that the good that is desired is possible to attain.

Thus, my description of this practice also assumes Aquinas's three remaining points about the object of hope being future, arduous, and yet possible of attainment. This description captures the tension that I am trying to maintain. In Aquinas's language, the object is neither a trifle that comes easily nor something that is impossible to attain.

Furthermore, my emphasis on the activity of this disposition is in keeping with Aquinas's classification of hope as an act of appetite rather than cognition. Classifying hope as an act of appetite is essential because of the connection between hope and agency. Hope is more than knowledge of the object; it is movement toward it. When I speak of the disposition of hope having a revolutionary sensibility, I try to convey this kind of momentum as well.

I also appreciate Aquinas's attention to the effect that experience has on hope. Recall his position that experience affects hope positively in two ways (by making an object possible or by making one perceive it to be so) and negatively in one way (by demonstrating that which one thought was possible is not so). Although only the positive experiences *cause* hope, all experiences affect it. I push this a bit more to say that all experiences teach us about hope. Even the experience that shows us that something is not possible instructs us about hope. How else could experience teach us that the object of hope is not yet and is arduous? Moreover, if we stress hope's distance from optimism, we might even see these negative experiences working *with* the positive to *cause* hope. Negative experiences cause hope rather than optimism because they confront us with the vulnerability of life. These experiences do not buoy the spirit, but they do steel it. The positive and negative experiences work together to sustain hope, true hope. The positive experience alone might sustain optimism/presumption, and the negative experience alone might sustain despair. But collectively, they cause hope, properly understood.

I do not see this difference concerning the effect of experience as a significant departure from the traditional concept of hope that Aquinas elaborated. Indeed, so far, my concept seems aligned with the tradition. The object of hope is not yet present, is arduous to attain, and yet is possible. Finally, experience teaches us about these qualities. The practice of negotiation is precisely intended to maintain our awareness of both difficulty and possibility and to sustain our labor on behalf of something not yet fully present.

Hope as a Theological Virtue

Here we turn to the *Treatise on the Virtues*, which describes hope as a virtue that is instilled in us by God and orients us toward God. In these articles, the appetite is structured as a habit or disposition; the object is clarified as the *summum bonum*; and hope's cause is determined to be God. In order to understand Aquinas's concept of virtue, we need to examine one of his informing sources, Aristotle's *Nicomachean Ethics*. Although scholars debate the exact date of these lectures, they seem to agree that Aristotle delivered them while teaching at the Lyceum in Athens between 335/4 and 323 B.C.E. [15] These materials then became available in Latin beginning in the middle of the twelfth century. [16] While many of his contemporaries rejected these pagan writings, Aquinas wove the philosopher's work together with Christian sources, thus earning him the nickname "The Great Synthesizer."

In these lectures that we know as *Nicomachean Ethics*, Aristotle describes the process of learning those "praiseworthy characteristics" that render one well disposed. [17] In the first book, Aristotle builds his telic position, beginning with the claim that all things act according to an end.

Every action is undertaken for some purpose and with a goal in mind. That goal, the end toward which one aims, is the good. Any good may be desired as a means toward something else, but, at some point, there must be an end desired for its own sake, "the highest good."[18] Aristotle posits happiness as the highest good for human beings. It is the end of our actions and deficient nothing; "happiness is something final and self-sufficient."[19] Concerned with sounding "trite," however, Aristotle makes one further suggestion, namely that we understand happiness as both well-being and well-doing.[20] That is, Aristotle asserts that the highest good is a functional excellence whereby the human being perfectly performs the function of being human.

From this starting point, Aristotle proceeds to identify those habits by which human beings attain happiness. These habits are the virtues, *aretē*. The end of human activity is conformity with virtue and thus functional excellence. Virtue is a characteristic or habit[21] (rather than an emotion or capacity) that "(1) renders good the thing itself of which it is the excellence, and (2) causes it to perform its function well. For example, the excellence of the eye makes both the eye and its function good, for good sight is due to the excellence of the eye."[22] Again, the emphasis is on the way in which these habits dispose one to act toward the end of functional excellence.

Some habits pertain to the intellect and owe their "origin and development chiefly to teaching."[23] Intellectual excellence therefore depends on experience and time. However, Aristotle suggests that the second type of virtue, pertaining to the moral life, is "formed by habit."[24] That is, intellectual virtues are learned by study while moral virtues are learned by action. We are, by nature, "equipped with the ability to receive" the moral virtues, writes Aristotle, but "habit brings this ability to completion and fulfillment."[25] Therefore, he continues, "we become just by the practice of just actions, self-controlled by exercising self-control, and courageous by performing acts of courage." [26] The opposite holds true also. We acquire bad, unjust, fearful, indulgent habits by performing those kinds of actions. In sum, "the actions determine what kind of characteristics are developed." [27] This means that moral virtues are not acquired by performing any kind of action, but only by performing those actions that a virtuous person would perform. Thus, learning the moral virtues involves deliberative activity. One must choose the virtuous act and thus cultivate the disposition to do so.

In the writings of Saint Augustine (one of the main Christian contributors to Aquinas's synthesis), we see a similar description of virtue as that which enables human beings to function properly. Augustine describes the virtues as those habits "by which men live rightly," in accordance with spiritual rather than temporal concerns. [28] For Augustine, the virtues ready a "disposition of the spirit which clings to immutable goods." [29] The end of all activity and the end toward which the virtues orient us is the happy life, in which the "desires of the flesh do not oppose the spirit." [30]

Augustine took issue with the suggestion that such happiness could be attained in this lifetime. In *City of God*, he sets out to expose the "hollow realities" of those who "endeavor to create happiness amidst the unhappiness of this life." [31] The end toward which human beings should orient their actions is union with God, something unattainable in earthly existence. The supreme good and final end is eternal peace and happiness.

> Even the righteous man himself will not live the life he wishes unless he reaches that state where he is wholly exempt from death, deception and distress, and has the assurance that he will forever be exempt... Therefore life will only be truly happy when it is eternal. [32]

According to Augustine, therefore, virtues are the habits by which we turn from earthly concerns toward God. By this orientation, and the habits that cultivate it, human beings function well and live rightly. But the end of this activity is only realized when life is eternal.

Saint Thomas Aquinas synthesized these two positions regarding the end of human life. Drawing from Aristotle, he argued that one can attain happiness with the help of intellectual and moral virtues. Speculative habits confer the capacity for good operation, and a moral virtue "brings about the good use of these speculative habits."[33] Through these virtues, human beings can realize happiness "proportioned to human nature."[34] Beyond the highest good attainable by human beings through natural means, however, there lies supernatural happiness.

> Now because happiness of this kind is beyond the capacity of human nature, man's natural principles, by which he proceeds to act well in proportion to his capacity, are not sufficient for ordering man to this happiness. Hence certain additional principles must be given by God to man by which he can thus be ordered to supernatural happiness.[35]

These are the theological virtues of faith, hope, and love.

As we have seen, the virtues are habits by which one is disposed to act well, according to a suitable end, be it natural or supernatural beatitude. But how does hope, in particular, dispose us to function excellently? Aristotle does not provide a direct answer to this question because he did not include hope in his treatment of the virtues. He does, however, make some suggestive comments about courage and optimism that will be considered later. Augustine does not address this question fully because his comments about the nature of hope are rather limited, focusing on the object of hope and in whom to hope. In the *Enchiridion*, for example, Augustine teaches that the Lord's Prayer is the proper expression of human hopes. In Matthew's version, there are three petitions for eternal goods and four petitions for temporal goods, he notes. The latter are necessary to this life, but the other three (one hopes) "will be an everlasting possession."[36] Throughout this text, the *Confessions*, and the *City of God*, Augustine's main concern about hope is that it must rest with God and not with human beings: "And all my hope is nowhere except in your great mercy."[37] The proper posture for hope, then, is captured in the prayer, "Thy will be done."

Aquinas, by contrast, devotes whole sections of the *Summa Theologiae* to an analytic discussion of the virtue of hope, providing a more complete answer to the question about its function. As mentioned earlier, Aquinas taught that theological virtues, like hope, dispose us to act well, according to the end of supernatural happiness. This means, in part, that one orients his or her activity to the goal of "enjoyment of God."[38] The individual is disposed to act in accordance with this end. The intention to act according to a particular end depends, in large part, on whether one deems that end to be possible. Left to natural inclinations, Aquinas points out, human beings may perceive the end of supernatural happiness to be impossible. The theological virtues, however, dispose one to "apprehend by faith what we hope for and love."[39] In short, these three things expand our sense of possibility.

The theological virtue of hope therefore infuses human beings with a sense that extraordinary and supernatural ends are attainable *with and through* God. And, most importantly, the *summum bonum* of life with God is apprehended by faith and thus made accessible through hope in God. This highest good, the end of all activity, is then the ultimate object of hope. The *basileia tou theou* is not hoped for as the means to something else. It is the greatest good. Thus, the virtue of hope enables us to function excellently because it orients us toward this highest good and, fused with faith, allows us to see this highest good as possible to attain.

Can We Hope in Excess?

The assurance that this highest good (or any good) is possible to attain raises a question at the heart of this book. Is it possible to hope in excess? Aristotle taught that all virtues observe a mean. That is, we practice a virtue by aiming toward the mean between excess and deficiency. Aquinas, however, argued that the theological virtues do not observe this mean. He writes, "Whenever a virtue consists in a mean, one can sin by excess as well as by defect. But it is not possible to sin by excess with respect to God, the object of theological virtue, for 'Blessing the Lord, exalt him as much as you can; for he is above all praise' (Ecclesiasticus 43:33). Therefore a theological virtue does not observe a mean." [40] As long as one hopes in God, one cannot hope in excess. However, the Christian tradition does warn against the sin of presumption, which suggests that hoping in excess is possible. But again, Aquinas teaches that although one may "be presumptuous insofar as he hopes for a good from God beyond his condition, ... there cannot be too much hope in relation to God." [41] Aquinas's response reflects Augustine's teaching here. The aim of Christian life is union with God; this is the central concern. One cannot hope for that union in excess.

Before delving more deeply into this question, it is necessary to review Aristotle's doctrine of the mean. Aristotle taught that virtues "are destroyed by excess and by deficiency and are preserved by the mean." [42] He thus referred to three dispositions: mean, excess, and deficiency. In every situation, the individual must intentionally act according to the mean, which entails an evaluation of the situation and one's own inclinations toward one of the two extremes. This implies that some kind of ongoing self-assessment is necessary. If, for example, I tend toward one extreme, then I must consciously pull harder toward the other in order to hit the mean, "as men do when they straighten warped timber."[43] In order to illustrate the mean and errors of particular virtues, Aristotle provided his students with a table that might have looked something like this:

Deficiency	Virtue	Excess
Cowardice	Courage	Recklessness
Insensitivity	Self-control	Self-indulgence
Stinginess	Generosity	Extravagance
Small-mindedness	High-mindedness	Vanity

Table 1. Aristotle's Doctrine of the Mean [44]

Aristotle described courage as the mean between fear and confidence, with the extremes being cowardice and recklessness. Later, in book three, he lends increased specificity to this definition. He reiterates his point that the virtue cannot be established arithmetically because it varies according to person and situation. In his words,

> the same things are not fearful to all people, and there are some things of which we say that they surpass human endurance. The latter are fearful at least to every sensible person. But terrors which are humanly bearable differ in magnitude and degree, and so do the circumstances that inspire confidence.... Accordingly, he is courageous who endures and fears the right things, for the right motive, in the right manner, and at the right time, and who displays confidence in a similar way. For a courageous man feels and acts according to the merits of each case and as reason guides him. [45]

Aristotle then turns to the types of excess, cowardice and recklessness. The reckless person fears nothing, "neither earthquake nor flood."[46] This person is boastful and puts on a show of confidence. In short, the reckless person's attitude shows no reflection upon or relation to the situation at hand. The disposition is not adopted through prudent evaluation of one's situation and one's own inclinations. It is simply a resolve to put on a brave face, regardless of the circumstances. In other words, recklessness involves a show of bravery in a situation that strikes fear in a sensible person. It is a show of confidence or bravado in a situation that surpasses human endurance. To the other extreme, a coward "fears the wrong things, in the wrong manner."[47] This person is utterly overwhelmed by a situation. "A coward is a pessimistic sort of fellow, for he fears everything. But a courageous man is the very opposite, because confidence implies optimism."[48]

Regarding the virtue of hope, Aquinas acknowledges the sins of presumption and despair, but denies the application of Aristotle's doctrine to the theological virtues. His argument rests on the measure or rule of virtue. Moral virtues regulate the passions, which is their matter, according to the rule of reason. In the case of courage, for example, reason determines the measure of courage, given the specific person and situation. Falling short of that measure constitutes deficiency; surpassing it constitutes excess.[49] Theological virtues, by contrast, have a twofold measure. The first, "taken from the very nature of ... theological virtue is God Himself."[50] Because this measure exceeds all human capability, we can never err in excess. In Aquinas's words, "we can never love God as much as He should be loved, nor believe or hope in Him as much as we should.... Accordingly, the good of such virtue does not consist in a mean; rather, the more one approaches the extreme of it the better one becomes."[51] The second measure of theological virtues is human, the measure of our condition. Thus, for example, "a man is said to be presumptuous insofar as he hopes for a good from God beyond his condition, or he is said to despair because he does not hope for what he could according to his condition." [52]

This question and Aquinas's distinction between hoping in God and hoping in human beings receive further attention in question 17 of the *secunda secundae*, which is devoted to "hope considered in itself." Article four considers "whether a man can lawfully hope in man." Aquinas begins his response by reminding us that hope "regards two things, viz. the good which it intends to obtain, and the help by which that good is obtained." He continues, "Now the good which a man hopes to obtain, has the aspect of a final cause, while the help by which one hopes to obtain that good, has the character of an efficient cause." [53] Each cause is further sub-divided between a principal and secondary cause. So, regarding the object which one hopes to attain, there is a principal end, which *is* the last end, and a secondary end, which *refers* to the last end. In parallel fashion, that which helps one to attain this good includes the principal efficient cause or first agent and the secondary efficient cause or instrumental agent. One may lawfully hope in the final cause of happiness and in the first agent helping to attain that final cause. However, one may only hope in the secondary cause and the instrumental agent insofar as they refer to the principal and primary. We may not, therefore, hope in any person as though he or she were the "first cause of movement toward happiness." [54] However, we may hope in persons as instrumental agents and correspondingly blame persons who prove untrustworthy as helpers. [55]

Aquinas builds on this distinction in the fifth article of this question in which he once again considers hope as a theological virtue. [56] Here, Aquinas acknowledges that hope may have many objects. However, he insists that hope is a theological and not a moral virtue because its objects refer to the last end, the principal, final cause, God. Properly understood,

all lawful objects of hope point toward God. Or we might say more collo-
quially, one measure of the virtuousness of hope is that its ultimate object
is God and that all other objects are understood and pursued only as
means to union with God. Finally, in this article, Aquinas once again
addresses the question of the mean directly by considering the following
objection: "Hope is a mean between presumption and despair. Therefore
hope is not a theological virtue."[57] Aquinas responds that hope "may
have a mean and extremes, as regards those things a man trusts to obtain,
insofar as he either presumes above his capability, or despairs of things of
which he is capable."[58] However, "hope has no mean or extremes, as
regards its principal object, since it is impossible to trust too much in the
Divine assistance."[59] Hope in and for God—hope with God as source and
object—cannot be excessive.

Let us push this point a bit more by asking why it is impossible to trust too
much in divine assistance.[60] Aquinas's answer is that God's power is infinite.
And God's power is infinite because God's essence has no limitations.
Consider human beings, by contrast. "The being of man is limited to the
species of man," taught Aquinas, "because it is received into the nature of
the human species."[61] Our essence has limitations of form. However, God is
pure being, an essence that is not confined to a container. God's being is not
"received into anything" and is thus not limited by any receptacle.[62]

What does it mean to say that God's power is infinite? Aquinas understood powers to be "in relation to act"[63] and manifested by effects or "spec-
ified by their exercises."[64] To describe such power as infinite, therefore,
means that there is no limit to the extent and intensity of effects manifested.[65] God's power never "produce[s] so many effects that it cannot produce more; nor does it ever act with such intensity, that it cannot act more
intensely."[66] Again, there are no limitations on this power because its
agent, God, is infinite essence.[67] This explains why we cannot "trust too much

in Divine assistance." It also helps us understand why the distinction between divine and human helpers is so important to Aquinas. We have to make this distinction so that we know where to place our trust, in whom to hope.

Also, this distinction between divine and human help is crucial because God's infinite power cannot be limited by cooperation with a finite creature. God acts *upon* human beings, not *with* human beings. Among natural creatures, there is "co-ordination," but "God is outside that order." [68] God does not cooperate with nature toward an end; rather God is the end. Here Aquinas employs an instructive analogy: nature is to God as "the army [is] to the commander-in-chief." [69] This analogy is instructive because it clarifies the unidirectional relationship between the God who orders (acts) and the creatures who are ordered (acted upon). Aquinas says quite clearly that God's infinite power has no corresponding power in nature. [70] Clearly liberationist language of co-laboring with God and feminist concepts of shared power are incompatible with this view. Both of these proposals presume a receptacle for God's infinite power. And the instant they do this, according to Aquinas, they taint what is perfect by limiting what is infinite. [71]

Because my proposal relies on a relational rather than unidirectional concept of power, I am furthest from Aquinas's argument at this point. However, there is still considerable overlap between my view and many aspects of this traditional account of hope. My description of the practice of hope as ongoing negotiation aligns with Aquinas's description of hope as an appetite or contending emotion that has as its object something that is good, not yet present, arduous yet possible to attain. Experience teaches us about these qualities. When we categorize hope as a virtue, my practice fits squarely with the description of moral virtues described by Aristotle. That is, hope is a habit that we cultivate through practice. And I assert that hope does indeed observe a mean between optimism and despair. Thus, we cultivate hope by preserving the tension between promising and sobering experiences.

In the analysis of hope as a theological virtue, some fissures appear. Augustine insisted that theological virtues orient us towards God, and because his God stood apart from the world, this orientation involves a redirected, heavenly gaze. If hope is theological and virtuous, it must be for God alone. Aquinas softened this a bit when he described worldly hopes as means to the beatific vision. Other hopes may also be virtuous as long as they are means to the *summum bonum*. Aquinas's discussion of the source of hope follows a similar pattern. We may hope in human helpers as secondary efficient causes, as instrumental agents. And this form of hope may indeed be excessive if we hope beyond the measure of human potential and capability. However, the virtue of hope must ultimately be rooted in God as the primary efficient cause and first agent. Hope rooted here cannot be excessive because God's power is infinite.

Thus, it is essential to this classic view that one's hope be properly ordered in terms of source and object. One may have many hopes and many helpers to that end. But the theological virtue of hope orders these many objects as means to the *summum bonum* of union with God, and it places ultimate trust in the unfailing power of God. The theological virtue of hope orders faith and history; it does not negotiate between them.

My proposal, however, departs from this view on two crucial points. First, I disagree with Augustine's argument that a theological virtue orients one toward God and away from the world. Because I understand God to be immanent as well as transcendent, such an orientation is impossible. When people orient themselves toward God, they orient themselves toward all of creation as well as the mysteries beyond our sense experience. They understand themselves to be a part of an interconnected web of being and that God's presence runs through every fiber and beyond.

Now, the beatific vision is a holistic one, involving the health of all of creation. This vision is indeed a vision of union with God, meaning the reunion of all that is separated. As a theological virtue, therefore, hope is distinct from any form of despair that doubts the presence of God and the potential for reunion and wholeness in each moment and place. When we lose hope, we lose a sense of God's presence. We also lose hope when we place parameters around its object. These parameters may correspond with self-interest, national interest, or even sense experience. Whatever their root, such parameters ignore the theological aspect of hope, which broadens our scope of vision. Hope as a *theological* virtue places our personal and otherwise limited desires into perspective. In this sense the theological virtue of hope is a check on egoism because it reminds us of the Whole in which we participate. Again, the orientation that hope provides is not a narrowed gaze in any one direction, but a broader scope of vision.

Allow me to reinforce the first point, however, because this latter one corresponds with arguments about the sins of pride and presumption that are more familiar. My first point is that we also lose hope when we deny or downplay God's presence with a particular place, person, or moment, even if we do so out of an attempt to avoid tribalism, pride, and presumption. We guard against presumption by orienting ourselves to the God in all of creation. And we guard against despair (or hiding) by reminding ourselves that we too are part of the creation in which God is present.[72]

To summarize this first point of departure, I agree that as a theological virtue hope orients us toward God. But I disagree that such an orientation requires us to distinguish between hope for God and hope for history or creation. Affirming God's presence within creation, as I do, dissolves such a distinction. One hopes for the reunion of the separated, the flourishing of creation; this is the beatific vision and *summum bonum*. Hope disposes us to act in accordance with this suitable end.

The second crucial point of departure from this tradition concerns the source of hope and particularly Aquinas's distinction between human and divine helpers. Because I understand God's power to be relational, I do not make a substantive distinction between divine and human helpers. Recall that Aquinas acknowledges that one relies on human help, can place hope there, and can blame that human helper who does not come through. However, these helpers are instrumental agents, and one must only hope in them as a secondary efficient cause. Because their power is limited, one's hope in them can be excessive. The first agent and the ultimate source of hope is God, whose power is infinite and does not fail. The theological virtue of hope does not observe a mean because one who hopes ultimately in God cannot hope in excess.

With many feminist and process theologians, I assert that God acts with creation rather than upon it, as though from a distance, or even through it, as though creation were a passive vessel. [73] This power is shared and persuasive rather than controlling and coercive. There is consequently no *substantive* distinction between God's power and human power; I cannot mark a line that separates them from one another, let alone place trust in one and not the other. This is, obviously, a corollary claim with the panentheistic understanding described above. As with God's presence, so God's power. If we understand God's power to be relational, to be shared with creation, then one hopes in God by hoping in creation also.

The main difference between Aquinas's understanding of power and relational power is that the latter requires mutuality. In order for change to be effected, all parties must cooperate. This understanding of power respects the freedom of each party. This is why feminists regularly contrast their concept of shared power to forms of domination and control, in which one party remains a passive participant. In models of shared power, no one is a secondary or instrumental agent passively carrying out the will of another. There is always the freedom to refuse the job, to resist the order, to say no. In process theology, God lures and influences, but does not exact a tyrannical will. Human beings have the freedom to say no, as well as the propensity to misunderstand or misappropriate God's influence. So, we cannot hope for change without hoping in human ability to discern God's influence accurately and in human will to respond appropriately. When the power that effects change is cooperative in nature, we must hope that all necessary parties will perform their functions well in order for that power to be realized.

Because I understand God's power to be relational, I do not root my hope in the unidirectional control of the commander-in-chief. Rather, my hope is rooted in God's unfailing and unlimited presence within creation, enlivening us, sustaining us, and nudging us toward realization of our potential. Moreover, my hope is rooted in our ability to know this presence and to respond to it appropriately.

As chapter 3 demonstrates, I understand God's influence to orient us toward the flourishing of the whole as our highest good. And I believe that we have an ability to cultivate a hope that disposes us to that suitable end. This hope requires two overarching things: (1) that we critically examine its many objects to ensure that they are in keeping with this larger good, and (2) that the source of hope not only sustains us but also calls us to act. Hope, rooted in relational power, does not assure us that the object will be realized. Rather, relational power convicts us with the fact of our own potential. The sense of possibility arises from a belief that I am capable of contributing to the effort, a confidence that others will labor with me, and a comfort that we will support one another through disappointments and loss.

Now I seem to be taking us down Pollyanna's road. Quite the contrary. I am fully cognizant of human potential for cruelty, but I insist that God relies on us, warts and all. This hope is not inflated by a romantic anthropology.

Rather it is tempered and steadied by a truly realistic one, one that engages our potential and our faults. This is why the practice of negotiation is so important and indeed unavoidable. In order to sustain this hope and be responsible to the world we know, we must hold in tension all of the contradictory truths about human nature and all of our contradictory experiences of God.

CHAPTER THREE

Contemporary Voices of Hope

My departures from the classical tradition place me in good company. I join social gospel and liberationist theologians who link eschatology and ethics by interpreting the *basileia* vision in social, political, and ecological terms that articulate a "hope for this life."[1] In order to do its job, to generate and sustain moral agency, hope must speak to the current condition of our planet and its people. And it must speak with a prophetic voice, criticizing the way things are and extending a vision for how they should be. That vision must be related enough to the current circumstances so that one can envision a path from here to there. Or, in Paul Tillich's words, there must be a "seed-like presence of that which is hoped for."[2] And it must be different enough to compel vigorous efforts for change. The object of hope must spark a revolutionary sensibility that the way things are is not the way they must be.

I also join feminist and process thinkers who understand the relationship between faith and history/creation in nondualistic and nonlinear terms. I understand the *basileia* vision to be underway, but not fully realized. It is an emerging reality. Construing the relationship between real and ideal this way affirms the real as a place pregnant with possibilities rather than disparaging it as a fallen creation or an in-between time. This planet and its people have potential that is not fully realized. The *basileia* vision is an image of our realized potential, and it is something to which we must give expression rather than a transcendent ideal that we approximate or a historical end point toward which we progress. Our work is like that of a sculptor chiseling away stone to release the form already there, or of a gardener clearing the debris so that the seedling can flourish.

My understanding of God's involvement in this process also bears the influence of feminist and process theologians. I hold a panentheistic understanding of God, meaning that God's spirit courses through this creation and beyond. Because I understand the spirit of God to be that which enlivens creation, it would be inconsistent to think of God as morally neutral or destructive. Thus, I assign moral qualities to God's involvement in the world. God is good and loving and at work in the world, creating space for freedom and enabling all creatures to flourish. Like many feminist and process thinkers, I understand God's power to be relational in form, such that God cannot effect change in the world if the world does not respond to God's influence. I also believe that human beings have the ability to discern God's loving influence and to respond to it with appropriate acts of compassion, solidarity, and works for freedom. Thus, the source of my hope—that in which my hope takes root— is simultaneously worldly and divine. I cannot hope in God without hoping in humanity.

In this chapter, I present the work of several twentieth-century Christian ethicists who have positively influenced my thinking on hope and the relationship between faith and lived experience, particularly

[handwritten margin note: Presbyterian put more hope in God & less in humanity]

Walter Rauschenbusch, Jürgen Moltmann, Rosemary Radford Ruether, Marjorie Suchocki, and Wendy Farley. I also reference figures whose work has been equally influential, but in a different way. Reinhold Niebuhr, James Gustafson, and Kathleen Sands keep me accountable to tragedy, and I use their writings to inspect my own for optimism, anthropocentrism, and idealized views of the Divine. These figures function like Picasso's *Charnel House* in that they temper my hope and prompt me to scrutinize my claims about God and the *basileia* vision. I value their essential words of caution, but I am glad that they are not the only theological influences I have. Like *First Steps*, the other theologians remind me that goodness and beauty are also aspects of lived experience. They also infuse my hope with an eschatological understanding that embraces the possibilities of things unseen, possibilities of the "hitherto non-existent and new."[3] Collectively, these figures keep me theologically responsible to tragedy and to the prophetic energy of the Christian faith.

I begin with a discussion of Walter Rauschenbusch and Reinhold Niebuhr because they are formative figures in the field of Christian ethics and because I cannot reflect on the relationship between faith and history without thinking about their work. Indeed, these two figures (among others) taught me what a Christian ethicist must do. My job is to examine critically the impact that Christian faith claims have on our behavior toward one another and the world. I am then to articulate the strengths and weaknesses of such claims and recommend alternatives in light of clearly articulated criteria. Moreover, Rauschenbusch and Niebuhr have a particular influence on this exercise in Christian ethics in that they have affected the way I understand and address the problem of hope. Their work assumes that the way in which one understands the relationship between faith and history affects one's ethical disposition in the world. Indeed, as young pastors, they both took on the responsibility of describing this relationship between faith and history *in order to culti-vate a certain effect*. Rauschenbusch aimed to encourage Christians to address the social crisis, and Niebuhr aimed to prevent their disillusion-ment. Similarly, my goal is to commend a form of hope that generates and sustains moral action in this world.

Paradigmatic Pair: Rauschenbusch and Niebuhr

One fruitful starting point for a comparison between Walter Rauschenbusch and Reinhold Niebuhr is their respective descriptions of religious experience. Rauschenbusch wrote and preached of a "religious energy, rising from the depth of that infinite spiritual life in which we all live and move and have our being."[4] This religious energy infuses not only the individual spirit but also society as a whole. Indeed, it finds expression in concrete socioeconomic developments. In 1913, Rauschenbusch per-ceived "a new shame and anger for oppression and meanness; a new love and pity for the young and frail whose slender shoulders bear our common weight; a new faith in human brotherhood; a new hope of a better day that is even now in sight"; a new sense of duty, openness to ideals, capacity for self-sacrifice, and an "enthusiastic turning toward real democracy."[5] Rauschenbusch argued that this new movement was the movement of God. He perceived in these socioeconomic developments a religious energy, a social redemption, or, in his words, the process of Christianizing the social order.

Reinhold Niebuhr's description of religious experience has quite a dif-ferent feel to it. Rather than an energy infusing and positively directing the social order, religion (Christianity in particular) is experienced as tension. Religious consciousness is awareness of what ought to be. But it is also the profound and sobering realization of a disjuncture between that ideal and one's real, historical situation. This awareness of what ought to be, as different from what is, propels moral action. In Niebuhr's words, "The dimension of depth in the consciousness of religion creates the tension between what is and what ought to be. It bends the bow from which every arrow of moral action flies."[6] Rather than energizing historical movements, Niebuhr's God convicts us with the ideal. From this tension arises the moral drive of life.

From Rauschenbusch, we have a sense that the Christian faith infuses all of life with energy, carrying it along toward the kingdom. We see here the influence of Rauschenbusch's evangelical, Baptist tradition. He placed great faith in the redemptive experience of an individual and of a society. He believed that Christianity was particularly suited to generate a more peaceful and just world. And he was convinced that individual Christians acting out their faith could usher in the kingdom of God. "I believe in the miraculous power of the human personality," he wrote toward the end of *Christianizing the Social Order*. "A mind set free by God and energized by a great purpose is an incomputable force.... Create a ganglion chain of redeemed personalities in a commonwealth, and all things become possible."[7]

Those who cast Rauschenbusch's theological anthropology as too optimistic overlook his insistence on the necessity of redemption. In an unpublished manuscript, entitled "Social Motives in Evangelism," Rauschenbusch argued that there must be a spiritual transformation to motivate and sustain social, economic, and political efforts toward a better society:

> We have heard so much about the progress of civilization that a serene faith has come over us that the cart is slowly but surely rolling up the hill, and that all that is necessary is to clear away the obstacles by

education and reform, and leave play to the inherent forces of humanity.... However evolution may work in the rest of creation, a new element enters in when it reaches the ethical nature of man. Ethically man sags downward by nature. It is ever easy to follow temptation and hard to resist it. The way that leads to destruction is always broad and its asphalt pavement is kept in perfect order, with toboggan slides at either side for those who prefer a steeper grade.... Let us not be beguiled by that seductive devil who tells us that man will walk into the millennium, if only you will point out to him where the millennium is and clear away the worst obstacles for him. Man was never built that way. If he is to get in, he will have to be lifted in. [8]

Rauschenbusch continued to fuel his thought, preaching, and writing with the evangelical spirit of his Baptist tradition. He believed that there must be an inner, spiritual transformation, enabling one to perceive God's activity in history, feel Jesus' social impetus, and labor for the *basileia*. Indeed, Rauschenbusch perceived a battle between the degenerative forces of the "Kingdom of Evil" (such as persistent social ills) and the regenerative forces of the kingdom of God. "The coming of the Kingdom of God will not be by peaceful development only," he wrote, "but by conflict with the Kingdom of Evil. We should estimate the power of sin too lightly if we forecast a smooth road." [9]

The intended effect of Rauschenbusch's work therefore was not to offer comfort and assurance, but to call for change in hearts and societal structures. Certainly, he was hopeful about the future and wanted his flock to feel encouraged as well. But he was also an evangelical, preaching redemption and transformation in the tradition of the German Baptists. Society will not be redeemed without a spiritual transformation. The social order must be Christianized. "My soul desire," he wrote in 1912, "has been to summon the Christian passion for justice and the Christian powers of love and mercy to do their share in redeeming our social order from its inherent wrongs." [10]

Reinhold Niebuhr also valued the ethical function of Christian ideals of love and the *basileia* vision, but he described this function differently. In his polemic against "sentimental liberalism," *Moral Man and Immoral Society*, Niebuhr described the kingdom of God as a "very valuable illusion" that gives birth to "ultrarational hopes and passions." [11] Without these things, "no society will ever have the courage to conquer despair and attempt the impossible." [12] Moral action, therefore, requires a response to this obligating ideal and acknowledgement of our historical distance from it. According to Niebuhr, we "must, like Moses, always perish outside the promised land. [We] can see what [we] cannot reach." [13] In their assessment of Niebuhr's dour prediction, many people overlook the importance he placed on the sight of the promised land. The sight and our distance from it instill a sense of obligation more compelling than a philosophical principle and more enduring than a naïve sense of optimism. These things provide us with a tension necessary to moral action.

In the work of Reinhold Niebuhr, one detects the influence of both the Lutheran and Reformed traditions that comprised the German Evangelical Synod in which he served as a pastor. There is, for example, greater emphasis on the transcendence of God and the sinfulness of humanity. God is related to the world just as the ideal, *basileia*, is related to history and just as love is related to justice. However, these relationships are absolutely vertical. God stands apart from the world as both creator and judge. The ideals, *basileia* and love, are related to historical acts of justice, but cannot be reduced to them. Religious experience is, therefore, not an invigorating and comforting energy, but rather a sense of humble gratitude and contrition. For Niebuhr, what one *feels* is not support but obligation.

Reinhold Niebuhr set out to temper hopes that he considered excessive, given the weight of sin and the tragic structure of existence. And
yet, given his goal of motivating moral action, a sense of the possible
remained crucial. For that reason, Niebuhr described an organic relationship between the ideal and the real, such that historical acts are not void
of significance. The relationship and distance between these elements
preserve the tension necessary to moral action. This pull fosters a sense of
agency by giving us the feeling that something is possible but not assured.
In Niebuhr's dialectical framework, human existence is shaped by possibilities as well as limitations. In *Nature and Destiny*, Niebuhr writes,

> On the one hand life in history must be recognized as filled with inde-
> terminate possibilities. There is no individual or interior spiritual situa-
> tion, no cultural or scientific task, and no social or political problem in
> which men do not face new possibilities of the good and the obligation
> to realize them. It means on the other hand that every effort and pre-
> tension to complete life, whether in collective or individual terms, that
> every desire to stand beyond the contradictions of history, or to elimi-
> nate the final corruptions of history must be disavowed. [14]

Because we face possibilities, we must not despair; because we face haz-
ards, we must remember "that history is not its own redeemer." [15]

In terms of sensibility, these two figures function like Picasso's two
paintings. Niebuhr gives theo-ethical expression to *The Charnel House*.
We die outside the promised land, and we need a Christian ethic that
responds to this reality. The work of this life is to prevent *The Charnel
House* by whatever means necessary, not to dream of "perpetual peace and
brotherhood." Our hope, in its content and form, must make sense inside
The Charnel House. Very valuable illusions do not suffice here. We need
a more realistic hope that prevents our "common enterprise from issuing
into complete disaster." [16]

First Steps reminds me that moments of kindness and acts of goodness are also part of historical reality. Paying attention to these moments restores hope in the human personality and in my own ability to effect positive change. Rauschenbusch's work has a similar effect because it calls to mind the countless individuals who address human need with relentless persistence every single day. His language of "Christianizing the social order" is inappropriate in a pluralistic society, of course. But the concept has value: it captures the idea that every day, in quiet ways, people are caring for one another by providing food, shelter, and comfort, thus following the moral example of Jesus, who cared about the most vulnerable members of society. In this sense Rauschenbusch is an absolutely essential counterpoint to Reinhold Niebuhr's more sober assessment of humanity. Empirical evidence, stories of "engaged goodness," demonstrate that human beings have the potential for loving actions.[17] Our hope must be accountable to *The Charnel House*, and our expectations for one another must be accountable to *First Steps*.

Hope for This Life

I situate myself in the trajectory of social gospel and liberation theology because I reject otherworldly visions that direct our attention away from this world and its problems, and I insist on a "hope for this life."[18] I absolutely agree with Moltmann's argument that an otherworldly gaze

> can deflect us from this life, with its pleasures and pains. It can make life here a transition, a step on the way to another life beyond—and by doing so it can make this life empty and void. It can draw love away from this life and direct it towards a life hereafter, spreading resignation in "this veil of tears." The thought of death and a life after death can

lead to fatalism and apathy, so that we only live life here half-heartedly, or just endure it and get through.[19]

We cannot talk about hope without talking about eschatology, but this turn to "the last things" threatens the very possibility of a responsible hope, one that generates and sustains moral action on behalf of this planet and its people. Walter Rauschenbusch saw this in his day, and he criticized the rising spirit of millenarianism for fostering "pessimism and world flight."[20] More recently, Christian ecofeminist theologian Elizabeth Johnson explains the danger this way: "By focusing on life to come in a distant place that is considered our true home, eschatology displaces our identity as 'earthlings' and undermines care for this planet, the only home we and future generations as living, historical beings actually have."[21] In other words, visions of another and more permanent and desirable existence above and beyond this one devalue this world and all that is in it. The person who subscribes to this view envisions the future—the desired future—as apart from the earth. Since the future rests elsewhere, the future of the planet seems less important. And, certainly, this is a rather benign sentiment compared to more apocalyptic views that anticipate the destruction of the earth as the dawn of God's reign.

Rosemary Radford Ruether suggests that this dualism is reinforced by an eschatological understanding that severs the tie between history and nature and thus envisions the culmination of human history in one salvific point at the end of a linear process.[22] Historical eschatology assumes an end to human history apart from the earth. It anticipates some development beyond history which either presupposes the end of creation or never even takes it into account. Indeed, there is a sense that human beings will reach their glory when all else passes away. In this way, historical eschatology "disregard[s] finite limits and relationships between humanity and the non-human environment." [23] It denies or discounts the interdependence of humankind and the natural world. In sum, Ruether criticizes historical eschatology for suggesting that the human race will reach its glory away from home. [24]

As a corrective to the other-worldly gaze, social gospel and liberationist theologians have consistently put forward interpretations of the *basileia* that offer a social, political, and eventually ecological vision for the world we know. For example, amidst the squalor of Hell's Kitchen, Walter Rauschenbusch envisioned the kingdom of God as a redeemed social order "in which the worth and freedom of every least human being will be honoured and protected; in which the brotherhood of man will be expressed in the common possession of the economic resources of society; and in which the spiritual good of humanity will be set high above the private profit interests of all materialistic groups." [25]

Writing from Peru in 1970, Gustavo Gutiérrez described the object of hope and its coming:

> The coming of the Kingdom, and the expectation of the *parousia* are also necessarily and inevitably historical, temporal, earthly, social, and material realities. The prophets announce a kingdom of peace. But peace presupposes the establishment of justice.... It presupposes the defense of the rights of the poor, punishment of the oppressors, a life free from the fear of being enslaved by others, the liberation of the oppressed.... The elimination of misery and exploitation is a sign of the coming of the Kingdom.... The struggle for a just world in which there is no oppression, servitude, or alienated work will signify the coming of the Kingdom. [26]

In North America a decade later, feminist theologian Rosemary Radford Ruether presented a vision of the new earth in *Sexism and God-Talk* that builds on this sociopolitical vision by adding feminist and ecological concerns as well.

> We seek a society that affirms the values of democratic participation, of the equal value of all persons as the basis for their civil equality and their equal access to the educational and work opportunities of the society. But more, we seek a democratic socialist society that dismantles sexist and class hierarchies, that restores ownership and management of work to the base communities of workers themselves, who then create networks of economic and political relationships. Still more, we seek a society built on organic community, in which the processes of childraising, of education, of work, of culture have been integrated to allow both men and women to share child nurturing and homemaking and also creative activity and decision making in the larger society. Still more, we seek an ecological society in which human and nonhuman ecological systems have been integrated into harmonious and mutually supportive, rather than antagonistic, relations. [27]

Visions like this generate and sustain moral action in the world because they connect that which is hoped for to that which *is* in a way that creates a constructive tension.

Moltmann describes the effect this way: "Present and future, experience and hope, stand in contradiction to each other in Christian eschatology, with the result that man is not brought into harmony and agreement with the given situation, but is drawn into the conflict between hope and experience." [28] This object of hope that relates to one's present experience becomes a goad to action. That is, one fosters the prophetic practice of criticizing the way things are and envisioning an alternative. As Moltmann explains,

> That is why faith, wherever it develops into hope, causes not rest but unrest, not patience but impatience. It does not calm the unquiet heart, but is itself this unquiet heart in man. Those who hope in Christ can no longer put up with reality as it is, but begin to suffer under it, to contradict

it. Peace with God means conflict with the world, for the goad of the promised future stabs inexorably into the flesh of every unfulfilled present.[29]

The hope expressed by liberation theologians generates moral action on behalf of this planet and its people because the *basileia* vision is both intimately connected to present reality *and* standing in opposition to it at the same time.

I situate myself in this trajectory of thought: I resist the otherworldly gaze; I insist on a hope for this life; and I value visions of the *basileia* that both connect to the world we know and set us in tension with it—i.e., visions that spark the revolutionary spirit that the way things are is not the way they must be. However, I have also been influenced by the work of North American Protestant James Gustafson whose theocentric ethics begins with a criticism of political theologies that construe faith claims with particular socioeconomic concerns in mind.

Gustafson provides a tempering influence on my own work, as indeed he has intended to do for contemporary theological ethics in general. In his "Response to Critics" of *Ethics from a Theocentric Perspective*, Gustafson identifies his intention "to force theologians to modify or correct exaggerated claims."[30] While he shares the cosmological focus of ecological theologians, Gustafson cannot abide by the liberationist tendency to conflate God's plan with a particular political or ecological agenda. Those who craft such proposals, he asserts, begin with political, sociological, or environmental concerns and forge a theological construal that meets those needs. "Religion is propagated for its utility value," and "God becomes an instrument in the service of human beings."[31] The proposals considered above would, therefore, fall under Gustafson's critical gaze because they are put forward with particular goals in mind, such as motivating moral action on behalf of the poor or among the oppressed. In Gustafson's words, such proposals are crafted and affirmed because of their "presumed beneficial effects on human attitudes." [32] Given my own explicitly stated concern about the impact of faith claims on the disposition of hope and my intent to construe faith claims so as to generate and sustain moral action in the world, Gustafson's criticism directly applies to my work.

Gustafson argues that such proposals do not conform to the way things really and ultimately are. From the sciences, we know that "human life is a part of nature, and dependent upon the process of nature." [33] We also know from biological and geological studies that our participation in this world, as a species, has been rather short-lived and remains insecure. Evidence from the sciences reveal that we were born into the cosmos, and our activity is circumscribed by its processes. This enlarged vision calls into question the "self- and species-interested conviction that the whole has come into being for our sake." [34] Human beings are not the crown of creation, but rather interdependent participants in it. Therefore, any construal that places human beings at the center of creation and in a privileged relationship with the Creator is inadequate, according to Gustafson, because it is incongruent with the way things really are. Aligned with this decentering claim is Gustafson's reminder that we neither control the processes of nature nor are privy to special concern from the Creator. Rather, the range of human experience, from psychology to astronomy, points to " 'powers and circumstances that are necessary conditions for human activity," powers that determine the limits and possibilities open to us. [35]

Thus, Gustafson continues, science and piety suggest that we cannot adequately assume that God's plan coincides with our well-being, in particular because such presumption is inconsistent with our place in the scheme of things. The more fitting disposition is a posture of piety before the divine governing and ordering of the world. Piety signifies "an attitude of reverence, awe, and respect which implies a sense of devotion and of duties and responsibilities as well." [36] Piety, as a disposition, therefore stands in stark contrast to the anthropocentric assumption that human beings are the measure of things. Indeed, for Gustafson, piety serves as an antidote to excessive theological claims and is therefore an essential element of theocentric ethics. This disposition is the "hinge which joins the frame of the moral and natural ordering of life to the door of human duties and obligations." [37]

Gustafson explains this moral posture more fully in the second volume of *Ethics from a Theocentric Perspective.* "A theocentric piety ... motivates and issues in a readiness to restrain particular [personal] interests for the sake of other persons, for communities and the larger world." [38] Therefore, the consequence of this theocentric ethic is that one consents to the positive *and* negative repercussions of this participation. In other words, the participant does not expect every development in the cosmos to benefit him or her personally and thus accepts the limitations of his or her situation as well as the possibilities it offers. Given the way things really and ultimately are, one must consent to the divine ordering of the world and to the possibilities and limitations of life. Therefore, Gustafson insists that it is irresponsible for Christian ethics to offer "'excessive' claims in the face of human misery, and give assurances which are not borne out by experience." [39]

I value Gustafson's warning tremendously. Like Reinhold Niebuhr, Gustafson is a voice to which I hold my proposals accountable because he raises several legitimate concerns. First, bearing the influence of his teacher, H. Richard Niebuhr, Gustafson cautions us about conflating a personal or political agenda with the "divine campaign" unfolding. [40] We cannot assume that God's will coincides with our best personal interest or best sociopolitical hopes. (Later, I will write about presumption that locates God's presence with me but denies God's presence everywhere else.) This is a mark of irresponsibility, and my concern with it reflects Gustafson's influence on me. I also value Gustafson's reminder that every action contains a mournful act. We cannot assume—or responsibly hope for—an outcome that is wholly good. Every event contains a mournful act, and responsible hope must attend to this tragic sensibility. When I write that a responsible hope does not deny the vulnerability of life, I have Gustafson in mind. Hopes that lose touch with this sense of vulnerability become optimistic and therefore irresponsible. Responsible hope remains accountable to tragedy and to the hopes of others that do not necessarily coincide with my own best interest. There is, then, an aspect of responsible hope that is perfectly consistent with Gustafson's posture of piety.

However, in my view, piety alone is not responsible hope, but rather constitutes one essential element of this more dynamic disposition. This hope responds humbly to the conviction that God's presence is everywhere, and it responds happily to the conviction that God's presence is also with me. Gustafson's theocentrism rests on a Reformed concept of God and God's relationship to the world that I do not share. For Gustafson, God is sovereign Other, an ineffable mystery to whom we respond with gratitude and contrition. Moreover, Gustafson insists that we cannot ascribe moral qualities to God's activity in the world because doing so is by necessity anthropocentric and anthropomorphic. My own theological viewpoint is much more panentheistic. I believe that God is thoroughly present in creation rather than a sovereign Other. I also join feminist and process theologians to understand God's power to be relational in nature, which means that we must understand God's movement in per-sonal ways and respond to it with personal actions. And I stand more with liberationist theologians who ascribe moral qualities to God, arguing that God is good and loving. My hope rests in a God who desires freedom rather than enslavement, safety rather than fear, love rather than hatred, peace rather than war, healthy and happy children rather than abused and neglected ones. Our theological claims must have moral content to be meaningful. And, in this world of absolute horror, God must be good to be worthy of worship.

I make these claims on the shoulders of countless liberation theolo-gians in a variety of contexts who insist that God's activity in the world has a particular moral quality that is known to us. God is neither absent, malevolent, nor utterly unknowable. Rather, God is at work in the world clearing space for freedom. And yet, Gustafson (like Reinhold Niebuhr and two figures yet to be discussed, Wendy Farley and Kathleen Sands) does press me to defend this claim in light of daily acts of cruelty. And I find that I can only defend it through a discussion of the relationship between faith and lived experience that parallels God's relationship to the world.

Faith and Experience, God and World

The Social Gospel movement purposefully envisioned history as pro-gressing toward the kingdom of God rather than existing in a permanently fallen and fixed plane utterly disconnected from the heavenly realm. "For protracted effort," Rauschenbusch argued, "human nature needs the sense of causation and continuity. It wants to see every step count, and the next step grow out of the preceding one." [41] Human effort is motivated by an image of development rather than catastrophe, he insisted. "This change from catastrophe to development is the most essential step to enable modern men to appreciate the Christian hope."[42]

Post–World War Two theologians who wanted to maintain the ethical function of the *basileia* vision conceived of the relationship between faith and history differently. Rather than moving toward an end point, they described the *basileia* vision as breaking in on history, as here and not yet. Thus, Moltmann insisted that "the Christian hope . . . is not a one-way street on which one leaves the present behind in order to flee into the future. It has two-way traffic, as it were. For it draws the future into the sufferings of the present."[43] Feminist and process theologians have continued to articulate a view of the relationship between faith and history/creation that is nonlinear and nondualistic. Their proposals inform my own understanding of a *basileia* vision that is an emerging reality we give expression to, rather than a historical end point we move toward or an impossible ideal that we imperfectly imitate.

Marjorie Hewitt Suchocki describes process eschatology by explaining process notions of God's interaction with the world. "From the Godward side of the dynamics, then, one would say that God receives the world in every moment of its completion. . . . From the worldward side of the dynamics, one would say that in every moment the world responds to many influences, the most important of which is the providential aim of God."[44] This is not a linear movement from the real toward the ideal. Rather, in every moment God takes up the world into Godself. And, in every moment, the world responds to the lure of God. Process eschatology describes a churning motion between history and *basileia*, real and ideal, world and God. These elements do not dissolve into one another, but rather exist in constant interaction with each other.

Suchocki affirms that the new community is already present in the world through the life of Jesus. But it is also present in God's own life and thus is not yet fully realized in the world. "We live," suggests Suchocki, "*from* the fullness of God's reign in Jesus, and *toward* the fullness of God's reign in God's own life." [45] But again, the movement from and toward is not a linear one, but a dynamic churning between the worldward and Godward side of the dynamics. History meets with, but never eclipses, the *basileia*. This means, among other things, that the reign of God is not fully realized within history. Suchocki explains, "The reign of God continuously calls us to a new future in history, and even if this future is actualized, God will transcend it once again with yet another call to anticipate God's reign in new ways." [46]

Rosemary Radford Ruether also describes the *basileia* vision as an ongoing labor. It is a continuous process of rebuilding ever more livable communities after ever-present injustice dismantles them. Ruether explains,

> I do not expect that we can finally develop or transform life on earth into a final, perfected state. This notion of final perfection is itself a contradiction of the finite nature of existence. I have come to think of our task of creating a just, peaceable society as a continual process of finding sustainable balances in a web of relationships of humans to one another and to our fellow creatures of nature.... The Jubilee tradition of Hebrew scripture is my model for this continual work of renewal in every generation, as opposed to the quest for a final revolution that will set things right 'once-for-all.' [47]

Ruether returns to the description of the Jubilee in Leviticus 25. This passage, she suggests, "teaches that there are certain basic elements that make up life as God intended it." [48] For example, every family has land and a fig tree, and neither people, land, nor animals are exploited or abused. However, the text continues, communities stray from this intended state. Consequently, periodic revolutionary transformations must occur to realize that intended, just balance. "This return to harmony within the covenant of creation is not a cyclical return to what existed in the past, however. Each new achievement of livable, humane balances will be different, based on new technologies and cultures, belonging to a new moment in time and place. It is a historical project that has to be undertaken again and again in changing circumstances."[49] Like Suchocki, Ruether insists that this labor is never complete. We are called to rededicate ourselves to labor on behalf of this vision again and again. And, as Suchocki asserts, the minute we glimpse the vision, it is transcended with God pulling us toward ever more loving actions.

These descriptions of the relationship between faith and lived experience, between God and the world, preserve the tension that is so crucial to responsible hope. They affirm God's involvement with history/creation and thus affirm the value of this world and the potential that resides in it. Yet these two theologians also maintain a revolutionary sensibility, insisting that we are called to be more than we currently are, as individuals and as communities. Their writings inspire moral action and enable one to sustain such work over the long term.

Indeed, Ruether describes a "different model of hope and change based on conversion or *metanoia*."[50] This conversion to one another and to the earth is not a once-and-for-all event. Rather, in the Jubilee pattern, it must be intentionally enacted again and again. One does not flee to the future, but readies her/himself for this "historical project . . . to be undertaken again and again in changing circumstances."[51] Ruether does not expect the *basileia* vision to be realized fully. Nor does she expect human beings to become permanently oriented toward laboring on behalf of it. Rather, she speaks of the "continual process of finding sustainable balances in a web of relationships." [52] Hope rests, then, with the "constant recovery of that Shalom of God/ess that holds us all together" and must be "reincarnated in social relationships again and again in new ways and new contexts by each generation." [53]

As noted earlier, Marjorie Suchocki also posits that the reign of God is never finalized but is always calling us forward toward increasingly caring and just actions. "There is no stopping point," she writes, "no time when a temporal reign is complete. No sooner do we achieve one form of God's reign than we must critique the achievement, and look again for God's leading, for the reign moves on." [54] Once aware of God's lure, a person is able to transcend the confines of his or her situation. As we have seen, political theologians celebrate this revolutionary sensibility and offer it as sustenance for liberation struggles.

In *Fall to Violence*, Suchocki describes such liberation in more personal language and thus offers another helpful description of hope. *Fall to Violence* is a text about freeing oneself from the entrapment of a violent situation and its clinging memories. Suchocki describes the suffering self as one who is absolutized, imprisoned, and absorbed in the past. The path to healing involves transcendence, which Suchocki carefully defines as an awareness of "infinite possibilities" that allow one to break free from the entrapment of past violence. The whole or healed self transcends the past, lives more connectedly in the present, and imagines an open future. [55] Furthermore, Suchocki affirms God's presence in this process as the one calling us "toward transcendence of unnecessary violence." [56] That is, God is present within this process of transcendence, luring one out of the absolutized and imprisoned existence and toward the open future of vast possibilities. [57]

Suchocki thus describes God's power as fundamentally relational. A key concept of my own understanding, this relationality forms the basis for my argument that we cannot hope in God without hoping in one another. In its form and function, God's power is persuasive and thus requires a response in order to have an effect in the world. As indicated earlier, I also believe God's power to have a certain quality such that we sense God's involvement in history not through any and every action, but through loving actions that resist suffering and enable flourishing. I owe this concept of God's power primarily to feminist theologian Wendy Farley, who presented a proposal for divine compassion in her 1990 text.

In *Tragic Vision and Divine Compassion*, Farley takes issue with the neatness of the Christian story that begins with a Fall to justify suffering as a consequence of sin and ends with "eschatological harmony." [58] This drama, she argues, quells legitimate outrage at injustice and violence by explaining suffering and promising a bright future. She insists that the more appropriate interpretive framework for lived experience is that of tragedy rather than a Fall. The tragic vision "retains the sharp edge of anger at the unfairness and destructiveness of suffering," she writes. [59] It insists that suffering is an unavoidable part of human existence and that it must be resisted at every opportunity. The tragic vision is not satisfied by speculations of a Fall or visions of eschatological harmony, but instead it demands historical justice and compassion.

The focal point of Farley's concern is radical suffering, which she defines as "an assault on one's personhood *as such*." [60] Like child abuse or political torture, this is a level of violence that utterly destroys an individual's spirit because it "assaults and degrades that about a person which makes her or him most human." [61] Such suffering cannot be explained away or atoned for. Moreover, there is no simple path to salvation, healing, or wholeness from these utterly destructive acts. Thus, Farley's corrective to this "strenuously antitragic" theology involves retrieving the tragic vision such that "unassuaged indignation and compassionate resistance replace theodicy's cool justifications of evil." [62]

The ethical response to radical suffering, asserts Farley, is compassion, which she describes as an expression of sympathy and love, a demand for justice and an empowering force that "mediates the courage to resist suffering." [63] This is an act by which one person buttresses another. It is also, Farley suggests, the most appropriate model for understanding God's response to radical suffering. Rather than locating God beyond this experience in a future, transcendent, harmonious eschatology, Farley suggests that God is present within the "essential hopelessness of history." [64] God's presence finds expression in acts of compassion and in the "actuality of resistance." [65] The power of God, therefore, lies not in transcendence from the weaknesses and losses in the world. Rather, God's power is compassion, the "resilience of the passion for justice that survives tragedy and in fact resists and defies it." [66] Similarly, the strength (and hope) of humanity rests not in a transcendent vision of salvation, but in a present act of compassion, the power to accompany another in sorrow and anger, demanding justice and resisting destruction. Through such practices, we embody a faith that Farley describes "as an ever-deepening sense of the long sorrow of the world together with a vision and enactment of the compassion of God for creation, a light always deeper than the darkness of evil." [67]

Sometimes, another's work gives such full expression to your thinking that it is difficult to identify the boundary between them. Farley's text has that effect on me. Her use of tragedy as the interpretive lens for lived experience is absolutely fitting. I understand her reasoning for it, and I appreciate the ethical posture that the tragic vision provides, namely the ability "to feel the grief of the world without being destroyed

by it." [68] I am recommending a hope that is in keeping with this posture, a hope that is accountable to tragedy, though not overwhelmed
by it. And Farley's description of divine compassion gives me a
foothold for talking about a source of hope that is simultaneously social
and theological.

Given my affinity with her work, therefore, it is particularly important
to mention another project that criticizes Farley for continuing to "strain
beyond this rent world to espy an ultimate identity of goodness and
power." [69] With this criticism articulated in *Escape from Paradise*,
Kathleen Sands joins Reinhold Niebuhr and James Gustafson as figures
to which my own work must be accountable.

Sands shares Farley's critique of traditional Christian theology as antitragic, but she puts forth a more radical constructive proposal. Farley
acknowledges the value of eschatological hope, but insists that it is not
sufficient. "Without denying the legitimacy of eschatological hopes," she
writes, "theology must seek historical response to evil." [70] Sands, however,
rejects all eschatological visions on the grounds that they assume either
the triumph over evil or at least the neat separation of good from evil.
From the beginning of her text, Sands challenges rationalist views that
cramp the world's variance into one uniform vision. There is no need "to
render reality as a single intelligible whole" and no justification for such
a view, she argues. [71] Similarly, Sands rejects dualist thought patterns that
are "moved by a hunger for a pure and unmixed good." [72] Through either
lens, tragedy is understood as opposed to life, rather than a part of it. We
try in all kinds of ways to contain, defeat, or redeem it. We try anything
to avoid the multiplicity and messiness of "world-questioning" tragedy.
These efforts issue in eschatological visions in which evil is either reha-
bilitated or destroyed. However, Sands insists that the messiness of

tragedy does not conform to uniformity or dualism. Rather, its "existential manyness" persists, and we must learn "to do without the closure of absolutes" and clean endings. [73]

The only response that is not antitragic, from Sands's point of view, is to allow the questions posed by tragedy to flow and unsettle. She therefore refuses to promise a divine goodness or to rely on "the closure of absolutes." Rather, she encourages a practice of placing one's own stories next to those of another, allowing them to be in conversation with each other and to raise persistent questions to the world. Her proposal is similar to Farley's insofar as laying down one's stories together is certainly an act of empathy and compassion. But Sands resists the notion that God also participates in this accompaniment.

Indeed, Sands challenges such "idealized views" of nature and the Divine, and argues that theology must resist them as well if it is to offer an appropriate response to tragedy. Rather than pointing to ideals, theologians in a postmodern age should reflect upon the complexities of the experiences of particular communities. They should not, therefore, refer to the *basileia* vision to inform hopes for the world. Nor should they refer to a model of divine compassion to direct conduct in the world, asserts Sands. Rather, theologians should respond to lived experience with lived experience. In her own text, therefore, Sands reflects on narratives by women as resources for these "vital and nonideal modes of meaning." [74] She not only meditates on these stories but also weaves her own memories in with the experiences of characters. For Sands, this practice of connecting with a story is as hopeful a practice as we can expect or should commend. Rather than envisioning perfect beginnings and endings, therefore, Sands locates hope in "our messy, multiform continuance." [75]

For both Farley and Sands, the promise of a happy ending is the starting point of the deconstructive effort rather than its resolution. While

Sands rejects any culminating image, however, Farley does affirm a particular vision of historical redemption not as "an otherworldly escape from history but a fulfillment of possibilities resident in it."[76] Though she resists the move to assure future well-being, she does affirm God's accompaniment in acts of resistance and compassion. And her faith in God's presence gives her hope—not that all will be well, but that one can stand in solidarity with those who suffer. There may not be the realization of a perfectly peaceful and just society, but there is a possibility, in each place and time, for resistance to the power of suffering. That is, in every context, there is the opportunity for compassion. And, according to Farley, God is present in every moment and place, engaged in such loving acts.

It is in these moments, therefore, that redemption takes place. Farley does not retrieve the notion of redemption as an explanation for suffering. Her entire project repels the claim that suffering is a necessary step to redemption. Rather, Farley retrieves and reconstructs the notion of redemption as an affirmation of possibility within history, not at its end. Farley does not envision a God who sits at the end of history, calling us to another, new creation. Rather, she understands God to be present within history and within the darkest moments of history, laboring "to penetrate the suffering and despair."[77] Hope, therefore, rests not in a future salvation, but in the copresence of God and other persons within lived painful experience. In those moments, one learns that evil is not absolute.[78]

Farley affirms God's loving presence and the possibility of redemption within a fundamentally tragic landscape. Sands argues that these theological affirmations betray antitragic intentions. Like Niebuhr's criticism of Rauschenbusch and Gustafson's criticism of liberationist theologians, Sands's criticism of Farley carries truth and implicates my own project.

I agree with Sands that affirming a loving God and an eschatological vision quiets the elemental questions raised by tragedy. This is precisely why I insist that a responsible hope must grapple with all elements of lived experience that call the promises of faith into question. This is precisely why I keep *The Charnel House* and Habakkuk's woes in front of me. Equally problematic for me, however, is the possibility that the tragic vision overwhelm the revolutionary sensibility that I find so important. Within the tragic landscape, one can only resist inevitable suffering. I do not minimize the importance of resistance, but I do insist that it is not sufficient for a responsible hope. Hope must not only enable resistance to suffering but also empower one to work for change. That is, hope must draw on the immediate strength offered through acts of compassion and on the prophetic visions that insist that a real change in circumstances is possible. We must resist what we know and also envision something else.

I resist the tragic vision here for the same reason that Moltmann resisted a dominant view of history that did not make room for anything unexpected. In *Theology of Hope*, Moltmann pointed out that we are accustomed to perceiving history as a closed system of occurrences that are either consistent with one another or at least connected through an abiding or constant element. It is this idea of and expectation for history that challenges the more mythical claims of the Christian story. For example, a view of the world as a closed system of consistent events cannot make sense of the resurrection and thus renders it unfathomable and contrary to all experience. In response, Moltmann recommended that theology must develop a new understanding of history, one that is broad enough to include not just the familiar and regular, but also the "incomparable, hitherto non-existent and new." [79]

Rather than restricting our purview to those things that are historically necessary and consistent, we expand our perspective to be open to the category of the absolutely new and contingent. Only with this sense of openness can one truly perceive the "eschatologically new fact of the resurrection of Christ. The resurrection of Christ does not mean a possibility within the world and its history, but a new possibility altogether for the world, for existence and for history." [80] In this way, the resurrection is a history-making event. It transforms history by disclosing an eschatological future and confirming the promise of God. The resurrection is thus historic not because it takes place *in* history but because it points to the future. [81] The problem of faith and history is therefore addressed *not* by adjusting faith to fit historical parameters, but rather by developing a concept of history that is open to contingency in the past and future. Thus, Moltmann puts forth "an eschatology of history . . . which revolves around the concepts of the new and the future." [82] Viewing history eschatologically means that one senses in the future a promise that is made known but never exhausted. Christian eschatology fosters a sense of hope rather than fear or anxiety precisely because the promise of the future is extended by a faithful God. "Hope's assurance springs from the credibility and faithfulness of the God of promise. Hope's knowledge recalls the faithfulness of this God in history and anticipates real fulfillment." [83]

I value Moltmann's eschatological view of history as an essential counterpoint to the tragic sensibility that sees lived experience as a closed system of possibilities. If hope is to generate and sustain moral action, it must be accountable to the tragic, and it must grapple honestly with the elemental questions that radical suffering unleashes. But it must also soar at times. Elsewhere, I have written about the prophetic imagination as that capacity we all have to envision something other than what is before us. [84] This is a crucial practice of hope. We must remain accountable to the way things are *and* envision alternatives that cultivate a revolutionary disposition.

Conclusion

The theologians referenced in this chapter constitute a significant portion of my intellectual inheritance. They do not have a monopoly on the ideas that I draw from them, nor are they the only figures who have influenced my thinking on hope. But they do illustrate the range of views that inform my position and the contradictory truths with which I work. Like Picasso's paintings and Habakkuk's text, these theologians have been my constant companions in this effort to understand the problem of hope and to commend a more responsible disposition. Chapter four presents my own understanding of the object and source of a responsible hope, which I offer as part of this ongoing conversation.

CHAPTER FOUR

Revisiting Hope's Object and Source

L et us begin with the observation that hope has many objects. Some of these are blatantly self-interested; others may be shared with a group; still others may genuinely transcend one's particular concerns. Some of our hopes are admittedly trivial while others warrant vigorous defense. Some hopes are passing, and others are nursed for years. For many of these hopes, it is possible to trace a progression of sorts, to see them as means to a larger end. When this happens, the seemingly selfish, trivial, and passing hopes take on greater meaning because of the larger good to which they contribute.

As we examine the object of hope in light of this greater good, the feeling of hope begins to take on a more formal and intentional character. I reflect on the ways in which my particular hope is related to yours, either cooperatively or competitively. I consider the ways in which my pursuit of this object impacts you positively or negatively. I ask what this object says about me as the one hoping. What sort of person do I become as I pursue this? Is that the kind of person I want to be? What if I pursue something else instead? Just in this brief and generalized series of questions, we can see how one moves from a feeling of hope to a deliberation about the relationship between an object of hope and the person one is becoming. This is the methodology of virtue ethics, wherein decisions are informed by the relationship between an action and character formation. As we move from hope as a daily feeling to hope as an intentionally cultivated virtue, we examine its many objects carefully and try to determine which ones are in keeping with the sort of person we want to be and with the sort of world we want to leave for future generations.

Before continuing with this examination, I do want to acknowledge the objects of hope that really do not connect to a grander purpose. We have any number of hopes that are simultaneously genuine and relatively trivial with a simple rationale. I hope my daughter sleeps through the night so that I can too. I hope that the meeting does not last too long so that I can finish getting ready for class. I hope that the rattle in my car is not serious because I do not have time for car trouble. Because my daughter and I are healthy; because my job is not utterly unmanageable or in jeopardy; because I could financially afford a car repair, these are relatively trivial hopes for me. I *could* connect these hopes to noble moral ends like a healthy family, vocational fulfillment, and stewardship of resources. But these hopes do not, truly, carry much moral weight. I simply want to be rested, well prepared, and on time. Further examination of these genuine though trivial hopes is silly, if not obsessive. My concern in this text rests not with trivial hopes, but with misdirected ones, those that are not directed toward a suitable end.

Now, here is the crux of the problem: what is a suitable end? Aristotle answered that a suitable end is functional excellence. That is, a human being should orient oneself so as to function excellently as a human being. This is both a helpful and very tricky starting place. I find it helpful because it prompts us to begin with an affirmation of the positive potential within human life, potential that resides in all of creation. Moreover, Aristotle's purpose of functional excellence correlates nicely with religious language about discernment and responding to a call. We begin with an affirmation of the potential—the possibility—within each life, and we set a course for its realization.

One danger with this starting point, however, is that it is also used in natural law arguments to restrict potential to physiology. By this reasoning, a woman who does not use her womb to bear children is not achieving functional excellence. Unfortunately, such reasoning finds daily employment in discussions about homosexuality, gender-appropriate behavior and professions, ethnic differences, and equal access for persons with disabilities. When I use functional excellence as a vision for human life, I mean one's realization of the fullness of humanity as a free, imaginative, and spirit-filled creature. I mean that she or he experiences well-being as well as well-doing. Any attempt to limit a person's pursuits or loves according to her or his physical form obstructs, rather than expresses, a vision of functional excellence.

A second danger with this starting point surfaces with the affirmation of freedom. It is entirely possible to set a course for oneself that disregards relationships with and responsibilities to others. Indeed, my own mainstream North American culture is steeped in the conviction that competitive pursuit of self-interest is exactly what functional excellence (read here success) requires. [1] We are indeed beings with free will and imaginative spirit, but we are also interdependent creatures of the cosmos. Our survival is wrapped up with that of others. We cannot, therefore, function at all, let alone excellently, in isolation. Functional excellence requires attention to shared needs and common goods. The suitable end for animals, like us, that are creatures of free will, imaginative spirit, and interdependent nature is an incredibly delicate and mysterious combination, namely a balance between individual needs and common goods. The *telos* is a flourishing whole, a system in which all creatures realize their potential. This is the suitable end for human beings in an interdependent system.

This proposal for our suitable end is informed not only by Aristotle and an ecological sensibility, but also by certain theological convictions that connect this vision of a flourishing whole to the *summum bonum* identified in the Christian tradition as the *basileia tou theou*. God is that which sustains life, and this sustenance takes many forms. It is the enlivening spirit coursing through creation. It is the energy to resist debilitating conditions, relationships, and practices. It is the solace that enables us to endure loss. We experience and respond to this sustaining spirit as we nurture, support, and comfort one another. That is, we experience God's sustaining presence through the compassion and love of others and through their acts of resistance and solidarity. And we respond to God's sustaining presence appropriately when we provide comfort for and stand in solidarity with others ourselves. But we also experience this presence through less tangible feelings, such as moments in which a weight lightens, anxiety subsides, or spirits are lifted— however subtly.

God's movement in the world entails creating, sustaining, and transforming conditions such that life can flourish. This is God's project, to use Sharon Ringe's language for the *basileia*. [2] The *basileia* vision is therefore an image that teems with life. It is a community in which human beings have their basic needs met and the positive conditions necessary to realize their full potential. We are free from inhibiting structures and free for self-realization, mutually rewarding relationships, and self-expression. We are liberated from present enslavements of all kinds and liberated for active, creative preparation for the future. We experience not only relief but also joy, not only satisfaction but also utter fulfillment, not only survival but also flourishing. [3]

This flourishing whole is what comes to mind when I read these familiar words from Isaiah.

> No more shall be heard in [Jerusalem] the sound of weeping and the cry of distress. No more shall there be in it an infant that lives but a few days or an old man who does not fill out his days. . . . They shall build houses and inhabit them; they shall plant vineyards and eat their fruit. . . . They shall not labor in vain, or bear children for calamity. (Isa. 65:19b, 20, 21, 23 RSV)

But there is more.

> For behold, I create Jerusalem a rejoicing, and her people a joy. . . . For like the days of a tree shall the days of my people be, and my chosen shall long enjoy the work of their hands. (Isa. 65:18b, 22b RSV)

This is more than survival and meeting basic needs though it certainly includes those things. This is a vision of plenty, of long life and even rejoicing. It is an image of flourishing. The prophet does not entreat his people to be relieved or satisfied, but to "be glad and rejoice for ever." [4] Isaiah's vision captures my highest hope of a world rejoicing.

Turning to the synoptic Gospels, one finds a variety of descriptions for this greatest hope. [5] In his 1976 text, *Jesus and the Language of the Kingdom*, Norman Perrin has argued that the *basileia tou theou* is a tensive symbol, one that has "a set of meanings that can neither be exhausted nor adequately expressed by any one referent."[6] Subsequent biblical scholars have argued that symbols require more "stability, permanence, and frequency" than references to the *basileia* actually offer. Thus, we must think of such references as metaphors instead.[7] Still others like Bruce Malina, argue that the kingdom of God is, "in origin, a political term," not a metaphor.[8] Malina, therefore, begins his exploration of the meaning of the *basileia* by asking: "To what sort of social problem was Jesus' proclamation of the kingdom of God meant to be a solution?"[9] Richard Horsley shares Malina's political focus to interpret Jesus as a political figure challenging imperial authority.[10]

I situate myself within the trajectory of social gospel and liberationist theologians who understand Jesus' ministry and teaching to have concrete social, political, and economic implications and to carry a special message of good news to the most vulnerable members of the population. I also appreciate linguistic analyses that call attention to the metaphorical and symbolic nature of language and thus caution against one-dimensional interpretations. And I recognize the contextual chasm that exists between first-century Palestine and twenty-first century North America.[11] Jesus' ministry does have a liberationist shape, and these texts should continue to offer good news to the oppressed. But we must be ever vigilant in our hermeneutical practices so that we do not oversimplify these multivalent images or overlook the contextual chasm. Julian Hartt's language of "construing belief" offers a way to keep the good news coming without committing either of these errors.[12] A construing belief functions as a lens through which we interpret historical events. When we do this meaning-making consciously and self-critically, it also prompts us to reconsider the belief itself. Thus, the influence is mutual. I make meaning of an experience in light of this faith claim, and the claim itself takes on new meaning through my experience.

I visited a good friend in El Salvador in 1996. We attended a march on International Workers' Day and marveled at the number and variety of unions present. I remember my friend describing the work of these activists as "creating space for freedom."[13] In a repressive regime, violence, fear, and silence work in tandem to keep a lid on disruptive movements. However, activists who refuse to stay silent begin to tear holes in that veil of oppression. And, when the repressive regime is toppled, these groups spill into the streets where they set about clearing the debris of authoritarianism and making space for freedom. The vision that motivates such organizations includes more than the absence of repression. It is a positive vision of a new community in which all persons may flourish. They envision a society in which all are freed from the debilitating effects of poverty and authoritarianism and freed for self-realization and active preparation for the future. They aim toward a community in which nothing inhibits a person's ability to realize his or her full potential.

Given my interpretation of the *basileia* vision, I perceive their efforts to resonate with God's project. Through the lens of this faith claim, I see the movement of God in their efforts to create and transform conditions such that all Salvadorans can flourish. From this point of view, for example, I would celebrate a free and fair election in this formerly totalitarian country as more than a positive political development. I construe such an occurrence as a glimpse of God's project. I certainly do not mean this in the narrow sense that God favors a democratic process. Rather, I construe such an event as part of God's work to create space for freedom. Thus, an experience like this points not to a transcendent ideal or future state, but to the *basileia* breaking in upon and rising from the here and now. Such a construal reflects Tillich's suggestion that the *basileia* "is coming here and now in every act of love, in every manifestation of truth, in every moment of joy, in every experience of the holy." [14]

This is how the construing belief works. However, the disposition of hope that I commend is not fully identified with this faith claim. It also remains accountable to aspects of lived experience that call those promising elements into question. Thus, for example, I do not get so carried away with the concept of creating space for freedom in El Salvador that I become oblivious to the post-war issues of land reform, globalization, and criminal violence. The sense of possibility does not block from view the forms of repression still entrenched there. Rather, I hold these things in tension: a sense that possibilities exist and an assessment of those ever-threatening structures.

Interpreting the *basileia* vision in terms of flourishing resonates profoundly with struggles for justice and freedom, but it is an ecological image as well as a political one. In this vision, the natural world also experiences freedom from exploitation and degradation and quite literally bursts forth with uninhibited life. A few years ago, I visited the Hall of Biodiversity in the American Museum of Natural History in New York City. There, I stood before the Spectrum of Life, a wall that is one hundred feet long and hosts fifteen hundred models and specimens of earth's species. [15] One can, of course, sense the flourishing of the planet in more natural ways, away from the cement of Manhattan. However, pacing along the Spectrum of Life was a poignant experience for me. Craning my neck to see those species way up high and trying to spot the differences among the lineup of pinecones, I was floored by the terrific variety of life, uninhibited.

Again, through the lens of this faith claim, the Spectrum of Life was a glimpse of the *basileia* vision. It gave me a sense for the earth's capacity so that I could begin to imagine the planet flourishing, truly teeming with life. However, one does not pace along that wall without a sense of ambiguity.

The Hall of Biodiversity is not just a celebration of the planet's potential. It is also a testament to ways in which human beings have impeded it. Through that display, one learns about the vast number of species already extinct and the rate at which human beings proceed to waste the earth. Thus, the visitor stands before that wall with a sense of wonder and mourning. As with the political example, then, the *basileia* vision does not necessarily overwhelm my awareness of the ways things really are.

To summarize this illustration, I interpret the *basileia* vision as an image of a flourishing people and planet. God is One who creates, sustains, and renews life continually. Through the lens of this faith claim, then, I interpret efforts to dismantle debilitating conditions as efforts that are consonant with, if not responding to, the spirit of God in the world. Similarly, I perceive certain moments to be glimpses of God's project, that flourishing creation. A successful small business breathes some life into an economically depressed neighborhood. A major pharmaceutical company donates research and drugs to treat parasitic infections in developing countries. Representatives from different religious and ethnic groups forge a more integrated political system. Uprooted persons return voluntarily and peacefully to their homes. Middle school students resolve a conflict through peer mediation. Survivors of domestic violence rebuild their lives. A green sprig takes hold in a blighted landscape. These are occurrences in which life asserts itself. And, through the lens of this faith claim, such occurrences suggest something of the movement of God and the approximation of God's project.

And yet, neighborhoods continue to deteriorate, diseases go untreated, ethnic conflicts rage and people are displaced, young people turn to violence and families remain steeped in it, and environmental degradation continues at breakneck speed. No lens of faith should take over our perception so that we are oblivious to persistent practices and conditions such as these. What we glimpse is a moment of possibility, not the assurance of a happy ending. What we feel is hope, not optimism. We must keep alive a sense that God's project persists against all odds like the mustard seed *and* that we must labor continuously on its behalf and be prepared to experience setbacks and defeat.

As I reflect critically on the object of hope, my primary concern is that it generate and sustain moral agency. As someone situated in the Christian tradition, it is also important to me that my concept of the *summum bonum* has scriptural warrant and theological integrity, and I have tried to demonstrate that in the preceding discussion. My primary concern, however, is a pragmatically ethical one. I am most concerned about the implications that this faith claim has for the disposition of hope and its ability to generate and sustain moral agency in and on behalf of the world. In order to motivate moral agency, the object of hope must be connected to the present in a way that *both* affirms the possibilities residing here and illuminates a path between that which is and that which might be. In his sermon, "The Right to Hope," Paul Tillich preached that foolish hope exists when there is no seed-like presence of that which is hoped for. [16] My concern is not so much with foolishness as with proposals that diminish one's ability to act. If there is no seed-like presence of that which is hoped for, then we have nothing on which to build, no affirmation of the potential in the present, and no "sense of causation and continuity" as Rauschenbusch rightly suggested we need. [17] These things are required to generate moral agency.

However, even more is required to sustain it. A seed-like presence, an affirmation of potential, and an illumined path are insufficient simply because an experience of loss, defeat, and disillusionment blows these things to the wind. In that moment of loss, the seed-like presence vanishes. In a moment of defeat, the potential dissipates. In a moment of disillusionment, the necessary means fall away beneath you. We tend to side-step these moments in discussions of hope, picking up the narrative again when one's sense of possibility, potential, and progress is restored. But if the virtue of hope cannot speak to the darkest moments in the narrative, then what good is it?

We cannot allow these moments to be the unmentionables in our narrative of hope because to do so disrespects those who suffer them. Moreover, these moments teach us about hope if we really pay attention to them. But the most meaningful lesson is neither of the ones I most often hear, namely that times of trial make us stronger or that things work out for the best. Times of trial, in fact, frequently leave us debilitated. And things do not always work out for the best, though people who are physically, mentally, and spiritually healthy are often able to make the best out of terrible outcomes. The meaningful lesson here is not really about human endurance, though that is encouraging. It is, rather, about the fragility of our hopes, the fragility of the common good, the fragility of God's project. The object of hope is not only something that one strives toward; it is also something that one vigorously defends every single day. In order to sustain this effort, we need more than a vision, affirmation, and illumined path. We need the assurance that we are not alone. In order to sustain moral agency, we need not only an object of hope with the qualities just described but also a source of hope that does not fail us.

The Source of Hope

This need for a source of hope that does not fail is precisely why many Christians make Aquinas's distinction between divine and human helpers. Perhaps their own experience bears witness to a world that disappoints and a God that does not. Perhaps they share the theological anthropology of Reinhold Niebuhr who warned us against placing hope in the broken reed of human virtue. But I have grown increasingly doubtful of our ability to distinguish in a meaningful way between divine and human help and increasingly troubled by a theological anthropology that insists such a distinction is necessary. Therefore, this proposal for hope roots itself in a relational concept of power that assumes, affirms, and encourages collaboration between God and humanity on behalf of the flourishing whole.

Every once in a while, experience places two occurrences side by side that inform one another and provide a sort of epiphany. This happened for me the weekend that I saw the documentary *March of the Penguins*[18] and then sang "O God, Our Help in Ages Past"[19] the following morning. This familiar hymn recognizes God as "our shelter from the stormy blast." Thanks to the documentary, I now have an image for that. Emperor penguins survive the blizzards of Antarctica by forming a mass, huddling together, and taking turns on the inside where it is warmest. Our shelter from the stormy blast is not a supernatural extension of power, but our inclination to huddle together to withstand the storm. God is there and there is power, but God's power is relational. We would freeze without other bodies to mediate God's warmth.

Relational power is even more than the mediation of divine power through animal form. Relational power presumes the agency of both involved parties rather than envisioning the power of one flowing through the other as water through a hose. Relational power actually affirms the autonomy of each party in a way that forms of domination do not. The obvious starting point in this system is an affirmation of the relatedness and interdependence of two beings, that they coexist and rely on one another. And yet, relational power insists that each party also has the autonomy to act independently of the will of the other. Relational power requires genuine cooperation, the mutual agreement of two beings to work together when they have the freedom to do otherwise.

This paradoxical affirmation of relationality and autonomy becomes even clearer when one considers the foil of domination. As Sharon Welch explains, domination is "the ability to act regardless of the response of others."[20] This form of power is characterized by a severely unequal relationship in which one party exerts his or her will over another who submits. As Welch so effectively demonstrates in *A Feminist Ethic of Risk*, liberal (as distinct from liberation) Christian theology affirms such an arrangement as proper for the divine-human relationship. "Doctrines of the sovereignty and omnipotence of God are meant to relativize human claims to power. Theologians argue that the value of such doctrines lies in their reminder of our lack of power and our dependence on God."[21] Submission to the will and power of God is the proper posture for human beings. However, Welch argues that deifying absolute power is theologically and ethically problematic. Theologically, it affirms an alienated and uncaring God who acts upon creation regardless of its response. Ethically, it legitimates imperialistic behavior on the part of human beings as well. That is, it lends theo-ethical support to the many ways human beings dominate others.

As a corrective, Welch and other liberationist theologians join many process thinkers in advancing a different model of divine power, one that affirms God's relationship with and concern for creation and establishes mutuality as a norm for human behavior. As Anna Case-Winters explains, the alternative to domination is "power that is 'power in relation,' empowering and working-with-other-powers (in synergy), allowing for both 'influence' and 'being influenced,' and persuasive rather than coercive in its exercise."[22] Working with others requires that one not only respect their autonomy and independent will but also remain open to being influenced by them. Similarly, persuasion requires the genuine and freely given consent of the other rather than the manipulation of a situation such that the person has no option but to comply. Relational power rests on—and keeps in place—two essential features of a flourishing human life: mutuality in relationships and the personal autonomy to make one's own decisions and act upon them.

Wendy Farley appreciates this turn toward relational power and away from forms of domination, but she argues that language of persuasion remains authoritative, if benignly so. [23] Moreover, she insists upon the need to specify further the direction or content of God's influence. [24] We need to say more about the "kind of power," that is, its content as well as its form. [25] To accomplish this, she turns to language of compassion. Building on her own understanding of power as "an efficacy for transformation," she describes compassion as a power that "mediates the courage to resist suffering." [26] Compassion, she writes, is an "empowering agent" [27] that enables one to resist both the causes of suffering and the "power of suffering to dominate sufferers." [28] She elaborates, "Compassion is the intensity of divine being as it enters into suffering, guilt, and evil to mediate the power to overcome them. As human beings and communities apprehend the presence of divine compassion for them and with them, they experience power to resist the degrading effects of suffering, to defy structures and policies that institutionalize injustice, and to confront their own guilt." [29] Like the more general description of relational power offered above, compassion prompts and enables a response, but it does not ensure one. In Farley's words, "The power of compassion is such that it cannot be absolute. . . . Compassion is an offer, a presence: it requires mutuality and relationship and therefore is contingent upon response. . . . Compassion is a condition for redemption but does not possess mechanical compulsion; it mediates healing power but does not determine a response."[30]

This preservation of the autonomy and dignity of the other to determine his or her own response raises a number of crucial points. When we insist on preserving one's freedom to say no, we cannot place our hope in the infinite and unidirectional power of a "commander-in-chief" any longer. Hope informed by a model of relational power *must* hope in the respondent as well, in the ability to discern this influence and respond to it appropriately. This hope is an affirmation of human potential to resist suffering, to act compassionately toward one another, to labor toward the flourishing of creation, and to sustain one another through loss. *And* this hope remains accountable to human pursuit of self-interest at the cost of others, to our potential for inexplicably heartless acts of cruelty, and to the moments every day when we turn away from the needs of the world. This is hope, not optimism. Because it persists in this world with an insistence that God *is* present and that we *do* have the ability to respond to divine compassion, this is hope, not despair. In its practice, as we will see in the final chapter, this hope takes on the sensibility of Sharon Welch's ethic of risk. It relentlessly persists without the belief that one can guarantee the efficacy of his or her actions.

The main argument against concepts of relational power is that they weaken God and exalt humanity. For example, echoing Aquinas in the previous chapter, one might argue that channeling God's power through nature—let alone requiring God to cooperate with nature—limits divine power. I think this is true. Relational power is limited because it relies on the participation of multiple parties. Indeed, I have not only insisted on preserving the other's freedom to say no to the influence but also that God cannot act without human participation.[31] Relational power preserves mutuality and requires the participation of both parties. But we

81 *did in the resurrection*

must be more exact. It is not that the amount of power is less; it is that the exercise of power is less efficient. We know this from experience: it takes longer to make decisions if one is seeking consensus. Because the process respects individual freedom, it is less efficient and easily thwarted by one uncooperative spirit. So, I do agree that relational power is more limited in the sense that it is less efficient than unidirectional control and domination. However, it is also the case that when a group commits to a single objective and organizes itself to work collaboratively through a division of labor, it can accomplish more than any one individual could do alone. But even then, the work remains vulnerable to glitches in the system, human and otherwise.

We should be clear that proponents of relational power models are not of one mind concerning the implications that this model has for our understanding of the extent and scope of God's power. Anna Case-Winters, for example, makes a case for preserving God's omnipotence in a relational system defining God's relational power as "the capacity to be influenced by *all* and to influence *all*." [32] Although she does not explicitly discuss relational power, A. Elaine Brown Crawford's transgenerational study of hope in the lives of African American women provides a crucial counterpoint to my proposal as well. Her book *Hope in the Holler* reveals a hope that is rooted *both* in God's empowerment of human beings and in God's ability to make a way out of no way. [33] Crawford describes the hope of African American women as "*enormous* in its ability to affirm humanity, proclaim their presence, and foster their ability to reach unrealized power, potential, and passion." [34] But she also insists that "their hope was a theological, as opposed to merely psychological or social, concept of hope." [35] This theological feature reveals itself in the lives of slave women, for example, who hoped in "God's care, love, and faithfulness *when no one else could be counted on.*" [36] That is, Crawford's study reveals a hope that is rooted in God's sustaining presence within humanity *and* in experiences with God's unmediated liberating presence amidst oppressive conditions.

Crawford's comments raise another important feature of the general concern about weakening God and exalting humanity, namely that such limitation on God's power denies the possibility of a miraculous occurrence. From this point of view, relational power weakens God because it assumes that only naturally mediated expressions of power are plausible. For the women Crawford describes, God's activity in the world may indeed be mediated through their work and that of others, but God's love, care, and support are also made known to them in spite of their immediate experiences of oppression, aloneness, and brutality. I do know that my theological claims are considerably more modest than many Womanist theologians and liberationists generally. And I suspect that I will not be able to convince some readers that mine is truly a theological as well as social hope. However, my turn toward relational power does not preclude miraculous experiences. That is, I do not see relational power and an openness to divine mystery as being inconsistent. One could certainly say that God's power cooperates with creation *and* that wondrous things happen. We can rely on something and remain open to something more. Indeed, I think many of us do both of these things daily. [37]

The other half of this overarching concern, namely exalting humanity, was presented in earlier discussions of Reinhold Niebuhr and James Gustafson in particular. However, I turn to H. Richard Niebuhr here to explore the question of trustworthiness more fully. The younger Niebuhr's writings on this point are particularly poignant because they were motivated, I believe, by a determination to survive disappointment. H. Richard's experience taught him that disappointment was unavoidable, and he assumed the responsibility of crafting a theology that would enable himself and others to survive.

As a young pastor, H. Richard witnessed the death of two young boys who fell through the ice during a youth group's winter camping trip. [38] He also struggled with depression in his adult life, including a hospitalization in 1944. [39] This experience and this illness, I believe, compounded the sobering historical developments that he and so many of his peers reflected on theologically. Thus, H. Richard's inaugural address as a new faculty member at Yale in 1931 was entitled, "Theology in an Age of Disillusionment." [40] He begins the lecture with a litany of disappointments, excluding his most personal experiences. He laments not only human failure to realize the hopes of liberal and romantic anthropologies but also the general acceptance of the pessimism about human nature that replaced those more hopeful views. [41] After discussing further disappointments in civilization, technology, business enterprise, church, and science, Niebuhr then suggests that the experience of disillusionment redirects our attention from that which disappoints to that which does not. "To speak of theology in a time of disillusionment may mean, therefore, that we can speak of a theology which does not ask us to adjust ourselves to the latest change in intellectual climate but of a theology which is forced by a change in the cultural outlook to turn away from the changing, transient flux of things to the permanent and abiding." [42] Indeed, he continues, "This renewed appreciation for the transcendence of the object of religion is probably the most characteristic and valuable feature of the theology of a day of disillusionment." [43]

Announcing a theme that he would pursue for most of his career, H. Richard argued that, in times of disillusionment, one discovers that he or she had placed trust in someone or something that proved unable to sustain that trust. H. Richard does not minimize the gravity of such a moment, but he does affirm it as a doorway to authentic faith. "The failure of the relative points us to the absolute and if it makes the discovery of the absolute more difficult it also makes it much more urgent. The revelation of the transiency of the transient points us to the permanent and requires us to find the anchorage of life in a rock of ages that is not in the age." [44] Twenty years later in the lectures that comprised *Radical Monotheism*, Niebuhr persisted with this argument, though he described the journey from transience to permanence in a more complex way. [45] One experiences disillusionment because he or she has placed complete trust in an untrustworthy source. After this disillusionment, the person flounders, placing trust in a variety of gods. This is the move from henotheism to polytheism. If resolution comes, it comes because the One is located beyond the many, the ultimate source of confidence, trust, and loyalty, thus exhibiting the radical faith of the radical monotheist.

There is a shift in Niebuhr's writing from language of transcendence to concepts of radical immanence. Thus, he refers to God in *Radical Monotheism* as the Principle of Being. [46] This shift softens the distinction between divine and human help. But substantively, Niebuhr insists that only the One beyond the many is worthy of trust. God is the ultimate cause and ultimate object of loyalty. This is the meaning of faith. [47] When we place this scholarship in its historical context, it becomes clear that H. Richard Niebuhr was crafting a theology not only in a time of disillusionment but also in a time of crusade. Against the backdrop of the Manchurian invasion, World War II, and the rise of McCarthyism, Niebuhr insisted that God is the ultimate cause, the "cause [that] transcends any community of selves." [48]

We continue to live amidst disillusionment and crusade, and our theology must also enable us to survive desperate times and to resist all attempts to conflate human agenda with the "divine campaign." But I am not convinced that insistence on the untrustworthiness of human nature is required to accomplish these goals. Quite the contrary. If we are to enable survival and resistance, we must mine these times for evidence of "engaged goodness."[49] And we must insist that such goodness reflects human potential and outlines human responsibility rather than humbly celebrating a momentary appearance of the Divine. Amidst the horror of the Holocaust, one finds the brave villagers in Le Chambon-sur-Lignon. During the years of repression, torture, and disappearance in Argentina, the Mothers of the Disappeared gathered weekly on the plaza. From sites of ethnic cleansing in Bosnia, one locates the Women in Black. In Rwanda, many found refuge in Paul Rusesabagina's hotel. In every place where hatred and fear fuel violence, one finds individuals who are determined to resist the cycle with compassion and love. In every refugee camp, there are people sacrificing their own comfort and security to help others. In the wake of every natural disaster, people risk their lives to pull others from flood, fire, and rubble. How can we learn about these people and *still* refuse to hope in humanity? How dare we do so?

As Sharon Welch explains, such stories of engaged goodness offer "no heroic pretensions, no grand narratives of certain triumph but a life-affirming refusal to submit to cynicism, alienation, and despair."[50] These stories provide a footing for hope precisely because they affirm the possibility of human goodness amidst cruelty. The historical context for these stories certainly diminishes confidence in the goodness of humankind, but the dangerous memories embedded in these contexts have the potential not only to restore that confidence but also to implicate those of us standing by. In order for this to happen, however, we need a theological anthropology that celebrates these figures as individuals who chose to collaborate with God on behalf of the flourishing whole rather than questionable creatures whom God managed to utilize in spite of themselves.

In order to survive and resist, we need a theology that affirms human potential to engage goodness and holds us responsible for doing so. We also need a theology that affirms God's unfailing and unbounded presence with all of creation such that the *theological* virtue of hope deepens and broadens our vision instead of redirecting our gaze.

One of the most important features of relational power as a source of hope is that it forces us to keep looking at the world even in our darkest hour. In a lovely essay called "High Tide in Tucson," Barbara Kingsolver writes,

> In my own worst seasons I've come back from the colorless world of despair by forcing myself to look hard, for a long time, at a single glorious thing: a flame of red geranium outside my bedroom window. And then another: my daughter in a yellow dress. And another: the perfect outline of a full, dark sphere behind the crescent moon. Until I learned to be in love with my life again. Like a stroke victim retraining new parts of the brain to grasp lost skills, I have taught myself joy, over and over again. [51]

This attentiveness practice, as my colleague Andy Dreitcer has taught me, is a practice of hope. And it is rendered theological by a concept of divine power as relational in nature. The elements of experience that bring us back to life are expressions of God's power in the world, a power that sustains and enlivens, and awaits our response.

CHAPTER FIVE

The Practice of Hope

W hen I first began working with this material as a doctoral student, I had not personally suffered any grave disappointments. I was fascinated by the material in chapter three of this text, fascinated with the way people construe the relationship between faith and history in order to cultivate a particular disposition. I had my research question, and I was off and running. I continue to find this question and the material discussed in these pages meaningful. But unlike my dissertation, this book is truly informed by personal experience as well.

During the fall and winter of 2002–03, I had two miscarriages. After ten years of marriage and as many moves due to graduate school and jobs, my husband, Tommy, and I finally felt stable enough to begin a family. After spending so many years of my life trying not to get pregnant, I honestly did not anticipate that this would be a difficult endeavor. I completely trusted my body to perform this function, to get pregnant and carry a healthy baby to term. Part of the trust in my body came from the experience of training for the New York City Marathon two years in a row. Tommy and I first ran it in the fall of 2001 and again the following year. Although I had always been athletic, I had never run long-distance, and I was amazed by my body's ability to keep going, as long as I kept it fueled and paced myself. I had never been so healthy and so confident in my physical abilities. After the second marathon, I realized that it had been a while since my last period. Training affects the menstrual cycle, but I was still considerably late. I took a pregnancy test and was surprised to get a positive result and admittedly relieved to have an excuse for my significantly slower time in the second marathon!

I was jubilant. I remember sitting in the sun in our backyard feeling a lovely combination of joy, peace, and anticipation that I had also felt on the day after our wedding. As on the honeymoon, I was filled with hope for the beginning of a new phase in life, and the anxieties and challenges that lay ahead had not yet announced themselves. We called my parents, and I learned for the first time that they had actually been looking forward to such an announcement! My remarkable parents and in-laws had never pushed the prospective grandparent question, and it wasn't until we shared the good news that I realized that they had all been hoping for this. We also called an obstetrician friend to get advice, and I quickly began searching for a good doctor, dealing with insurance, and making appointments. Then, just a few days later, I noticed blood after going to the bathroom. I felt a weight descend on me, beginning with my head and moving down through my whole body. Within a moment, the joy, peace, and sense of anticipation vanished.

Weeks passed, my professional habits kicked in, and I began to study miscarriages. I learned how commonplace early miscarriages really are. Even though studies were contradictory about these things, I decided to cut out caffeine, moderate my exercise, be careful to get plenty of sleep, and to eat well. And I took my prenatal vitamins religiously. I also began talking with other women who had miscarriages, many of whom had several and much later along than mine. In short, I began training. I trained my body for pregnancy just like I had trained it for the marathons. That confidence in my body returned rather quickly. I knew more, and I developed a guarded hope. I knew that further miscarriages were possible, but I also believed I had prepared my body well for a successful pregnancy.

The pattern repeated itself. I got pregnant again and began bleeding within the first month. The weight descended, but reading and talking with others did not lift it. I began to believe and to say that something I had always thought possible might not be "in the cards." I had already scheduled a doctor's appointment that was to be my first prenatal visit. I waited in the waiting room with other women, some of whom had beautiful round bellies. When my name was called, I walked down the hall, with its walls papered by baby pictures. While waiting for my doctor, I sat staring at an illustration of a growing fetus. When my doctor came in, he warmly embraced my hand, saying, "Ah, congratulations!" I awkwardly told him what happened. After a moment and a look of consolation, he patted my knee and said, "OK, it's time for me to do my homework." He ordered lab work and wrote out a prescription for Clomid.

During this time, some of the people in whom I confided tried to reassure me with the assertion that things work out for the best. I appreciated their sympathy and support, but this sentiment bothered me. And I began to assert something else: that sometimes things do not work out for the best, but people who are emotionally and mentally healthy are able to make the best out of bad circumstances. That is what I tried to do. I continued to study, listened to my doctor, relied on my supportive family, developed a friendship with a woman who had multiple miscarriages before a healthy pregnancy, and reestablished a connection with someone in the middle of the *in vitro* fertilization process. And, at some point, I decided that although biological children might not be in the cards for us, it was not time to give up yet.

I spent the first few months of the third pregnancy nervously preparing myself for bad news. I did everything I knew to do to protect this vulnerable embryo, but I also knew that I could not control the process. I held onto a hope for something that I could not ensure. I could not trust my body. I had no confidence in my womb. Each time I went to the bathroom, I held my breath, fearful that I would find blood again. But there was no blood, and my HCG and progesterone levels climbed. [1] At seven weeks, Tommy and I went for an ultrasound and saw the heart beating. I began to feel joy again, though not peace necessarily. I remained anxious and cautious. At some point, I simply became tired, and I knew that this little life had a good grip on me. Katherine Rockey Marshall was born on January 22, 2004.

I do not know how I would make meaning of the miscarriages if I did not have a healthy third pregnancy. I do know, though, I have tried not to let Katherine's arrival gloss over the pain of the miscarriages because they gave me a window into the experience of people who feel betrayed by their bodies and perhaps by God. Another friend has made meaning of her miscarriage by saying, "Without that miscarriage, I wouldn't have had Alex," her son. I appreciate her point, but my miscarriages are not meaningful to me as preludes to Katherine. They are meaningful because they keep me accountable to the vulnerability of life. In those months, I experienced an ounce of the anxiety and fear that so many people feel as they nurture a fragile life. I experienced momentarily a sense of despair that so many others live with daily. I experienced temporarily the aloneness and confusion of someone confronted with an illness and struggling to comprehend it. And on my darkest mornings, I felt the rage that haunts those who experience an unfair God, one who turned my babies to blood while giving children to people who beat, neglect, and abandon them.

I also experienced the grace of friends and strangers. My husband comforted and reassured me every day, gathered information alongside mine, and attended every prenatal checkup he could. My friend who had so many miscarriages herself often waited outside the women's restroom at work. Another friend took me to the hospital for a D&C procedure, and when we came home she walked my dog and called my parents for me. Throughout the experiences, the nurses offered a standard refrain that was oddly and consistently comforting, "I'm sorry this has happened to you." I met people who were crushed by significantly greater disappointment and struggling to find hope again. And I met people who continued to practice hope as they pursued a variety of possibilities for having a family. The miscarriages are meaningful because they surrounded me with testaments to the vulnerability and the resiliency of life. They are also meaningful because they enable me to assert without question that sometimes the object of hope is not something that we strive toward as much as something that we vigorously defend each and every day.

In Tillich's language, we find the "seed-like presence of that which is hoped for" and we practice hope by nurturing it. [2] We learn what this seed requires for growth, and we do everything in our power to provide for it and to defend it from threat. The second miscarriage was so much more difficult than the first because I not only felt the loss of that future child but also feared that the possibility of parenthood was closed to me. In my sadness, I confused the "seed-like presence" with "that which is hoped for." What I really hoped for was the experience of mothering, the experience of caring for someone and watching a baby grow into a person. My sadness diminished and my hope increased because of what I learned and because of the relationships I formed. I clarified the object of hope and identified many kinds of seed-like presence. Women who had multiple miscarriages before a healthy pregnancy became a seed-like presence for me. Foster parents and adoptive parents became a seed-like presence for me. But even more than that, friends without children who live happy and fulfilling lives became a seed-like presence of hope for me because they signaled to me that I could survive and maybe even flourish without realizing this hope of mothering.

One reason for hope's endurance is its elasticity. That is, hope is a remarkably dynamic disposition because it responds to possibilities that range from radical, positive change to surviving disappointment. A recent news story makes this point well. Marine Parents is a web-based support group created by Tracy Della Vecchia during the first wave of the second Iraq War. A segment on NBC's *Nightly News* told the story of Georgette Frank, a mother who was an active participant in the e-mail exchanges until her son was killed in action in April 2004. After his death, she stopped posting to the group because she thought she represented the other parents' worst fear. However, after responding to the numerous appeals for her return, she learned that she symbolized something else for them: "That they can go on, and their life can have meaning."[3] Hope has endurance because it is elastic. And it is elastic because possibilities range from a happy reunion with a healthy child to going on after his death.

Practicing hope, then, entails openness to reevaluating its object and searching out fresh evidence of its possibility. Reevaluating the object of hope is the most difficult part because it entails the death of a deeply held desire. One person with whom I connected in these months was a man who had spent several years with his wife trying to become pregnant. After three attempts at *in vitro* fertilization, they finally decided to stop pursuing biological children. Those of us who have not had this experience have no idea of the tremendous pain that this decision causes. This couple had been planning on biological children since they met, and had long ago named them. So, the decision to stop trying for biological children felt like a death to him. After they made this decision, he went to a lake and "buried" their children.

The practice of reevaluating an object of hope is heart-wrenching, but it is necessary for survival after disappointment because it illumines other possibilities that we lose sight of in our pursuit and pain. It is also, miraculously, something that human beings are capable of doing. We see this time and time again. A man allows a loved one to die because he determines to hope for his or her peaceful death rather than more life together. A veteran of war determines to hope for equal opportunity and respect rather than the full restoration of his able body. A survivor of a forest fire determines to hope for the emotional and financial resources necessary to relocate rather than rebuild the family home. Relatives determine to hope for the recovery of a body rather than reunion with a loved one.

We frequently describe the moment of adjusting a hope as "letting go," but this phrase seems an insufficient description to me. The truly pivotal moment is not so much an experience of letting go as of holding on to something else. Many babies transition between pulling themselves up and walking with a developmental period called "cruising." That is, they move around the room by cruising from the couch to the coffee table to a chair to a helper's hand and finally, in our case, to an unbelievably patient dog. Every once in a while, they rely on a ball that rolls or a not-so-patient dog that moves or a chair that rocks. But quickly they learn to identify the objects they can rely on. The metaphor of cruising is a helpful and, I believe, accurate description of this period when we reevaluate our hope. We do not let go and stand unassisted. Rather, we reach out for other things to keep us upright and learn, often painfully, which ones can sustain our weight. Then, we cruise among supportive structures—friends and strangers who have had similar experiences; doctors and counselors who clarify alternatives; music, art, and nature that sustain the soul; and faith that provides comfort and sustenance. Maybe one day we do indeed stand unassisted and even strong enough to provide support for another. But in the particular period of reevaluation, cruising becomes a practice of hope.

I suspect that H. Richard Niebuhr would critically describe this period of cruising as polytheism and urge me to place confidence in the One beyond this many. I appreciate his perception of God in each of these supportive structures, but I do not find it idolatrous to affirm each structure as collaborating with rather than more passively channeling God. I do not agree that faithfulness requires me to trust in the God within my friend rather than in my friend, or to find comfort in the God beyond the music rather than the music. However, such a distinction was essential to Niebuhr because of a deeply troubling aspect of his radical faith, namely his insistence that God acts on us through *every* action upon us. Niebuhr insisted that we could not parcel out God's action as only mediated through the positive experiences we have. We must, he taught, interpret *every* action upon us as God's action. The miscarriage, the death of a loved one, the war that destroys our bodies and steals our children, the fire that turns our homes to ashes, and the floods that sweep away our friends—God acts upon us through these things, and we survive them by realizing that God is their agent and that God is working, ultimately, for good.

I do not share Niebuhr's faith. I do not believe that everything that happens is of God, nor do I believe that faith and hope require humble acceptance of suffering as part of an unknowable divine process. I find God's movement in the world to have a particular quality. God moves us toward flourishing, and we have the freedom to respond to and resist that movement. The restoration of hope does not require a faith in a God who hurts us for our own good. Rather, it requires receptivity to the hand that is on our back as we grieve. And the practice of hope does not require faith that acquiesces to all as an act of God. Rather, the practice of hope requires that we discern and join the life-giving movement of God within this death-dealing world.

But how do we discern this movement? And, more concretely, how do I ensure that something I hope for is in keeping with it? And, when necessary, how do I know when and in what way to adjust my hope? The language of negotiation is helpful precisely because the answer to these questions is not clear. And the language of practice is essential because we cannot determine the answer without action, dialogue, prayer, and study. However, there are some parameters for our negotiation and our practice.

Drawing on an Aristotelian concept of the *telos*, scriptural imagery for the *basileia*, contemporary liberationist commitments to the most vulnerable members of creation, panentheistic theology, feminist understanding of relational power, and personal experience, I suggest that hope is virtuous when it orients us toward the flourishing whole, empowers us to labor on its behalf, and sustains us in the meantime. In order to accomplish this, hope must be rooted in a God whose presence never fails and has no boundaries. The object of a virtuous hope is the common good that includes, but is not restricted to, my personal well-being. In order to accomplish its task, hope must also be rooted in a relational concept of power that generates and sustains moral agency with its assertion that a flourishing whole is a collaborative endeavor and requires our participation. In order for this participation to be sustained, the object of hope must also illumine a path in its direction. That is, there must be a seed-like presence of that which is hoped for, something that enables us to cruise, to rest, and to regain our strength. And all of this must take place with attention to the vulnerability of life. We practice hope with one hand on a sustaining structure and one hand on miscarriage.

These parameters signal several ways in which we might err in hope. Clearly Aristotle's doctrine of the mean lurks in the background here. But the errors of hope are not so much in terms of quantity as in terms of quality. Moreover, we can err in multiple directions, not only in the directions of excess and deficiency. For example, we err in hope when we upset the balance between individual needs and the common good. Hope is virtuous when its object is the well-being of the whole. Therefore, I err when I hope only for my own good or the good of my group apart from all else. I also err when I sacrifice my own well-being for the good of the whole. Of course, this point flies in the face of our best heroic stories as well as other virtues that the Christian tradition extends to us. But hope is virtuous when it orients us toward the flourishing *whole*, and this requires me to see my well-being as wrapped up with yours, not something to be sacrificed on your behalf. In the language of conflict resolution training, practicing hope requires identifying shared interests rather than advancing individual positions. And we can only identify shared interests when you and I articulate our needs. Thus, we err in hope when we upset this balance between individual needs and the common good.

We also err in hope when we deny God's unfailing and unbounded presence. Self-sacrifice and self-interest have a theological dimension. I sacrifice my own needs when I lose a sense of God's presence with me. I fall to despair and do not defend my life and hopes as worthy of anyone's effort, let alone God's attention. And, at the other extreme, I advance my own interest apart from and even at the expense of others when I lose a sense of God's unbounded presence. If I lose a sense of God's presence with me, I fall to despair. If I lose a sense of God's presence every place else, I fall to self-interest, presumption, and crusade.

We err in hope when we deny the necessity of a "seed-like presence of that which is hoped for." I mentioned this before, but it bears repeating here. Without a seed-like presence, we lose a connection between our current circumstances and that which we hope for. A seed-like presence not only signals real possibility but also provides a stepping-stone or at least a place of respite. We practice hope by a realistic assessment of our present circumstances. And a realistic assessment involves looking honestly and thoroughly at the obstacles and the alternatives present with us. There is no way to practice a hope for this world without being attentive to the promise and the peril that reside here. If we fail to unearth the possibilities, then our hope no longer generates and sustains moral action. It turns rather to quietism or passive acceptance of the way things are rather than a vigorous defense of the possibilities for change. And if we fail to attend to the vulnerability of each possibility, then our hope turns to optimism that glosses over the tragedies of our neighbors and cannot sustain us through our own.

In sum, hope is a dynamic disposition that responds to possibilities that range from radical change to surviving disappointment. In daily experience, hope has many objects, but when intentionally cultivated as a virtue, the object of hope is the flourishing of the whole. We err in hope by denying God's presence with us, denying God's presence everywhere else, denying the necessity of a "seed-like presence of that which is hoped for," and denying the vulnerability of life. Hope is virtuous—and theologically so—when it orients us toward the flourishing whole, empowers us to strive toward it, and sustains us in the meantime.

What does this look like exactly? How do we practice this disposition that is so filled with paradox and balance? Like Aristotle, I believe that virtues do not have only one form of expression, one shape, one posture. Rather, a virtue like hope takes multiple forms depending on the person who practices it and the context in which he or she labors. Sometimes, hope assumes the form of Habakkuk standing stubbornly by the barren fig tree. And sometimes, hope assumes the form of a man standing sadly at the lake's edge ritually "burying" his children. We love to tell the stories of Habakkuk, of course. We celebrate the bravery and the faithfulness of these protagonists who do not give up. However, given the person and the context, changing that which is hoped for can be as virtuous—indeed as brave and faithful—as holding on to it. Because different circumstances require different postures, I believe that we learn hope by practicing it. That is, I turn back to Aristotle's understanding of a moral virtue as that which we learn by doing rather than Aquinas's understanding of a theological virtue as that which is infused in us by God. Hope requires such a delicate balance that it must be practiced, and the practice of hope is a spiritual as well as a moral endeavor.

Additional Practices of Hope

As I write this closing chapter, thousands of people are dying, grieving, and raging along the Gulf Coast in the wake of Hurricane Katrina. And during the week that my nation's focus has been on this devastated region and people, more than eight hundred Shiite pilgrims were killed in Baghdad when rumors of a suicide bomber sent panic through the crowd. [4] This week also marked the first anniversary of a horrendous hostage situation that ended when soldiers killed 186 schoolchildren, along with some parents and teachers and the Chechen rebels who had held them all captive for ten days. And these reported tragedies do not begin to capture the extent of personal loss that individuals experience daily as they struggle with illness, poverty, fear, intractable conflict, and abuse. If we who have the luxury to reflect and write about the virtue of hope cannot say anything meaningful and honest to people in the midst of their suffering, then our work is for naught. And we cannot say anything meaningful and honest without acknowledging their sense of abandonment, their legitimate reasons to despair, and their rage against God and the world of healthy, secure, and apathetic bystanders.

For a few years before graduate school, I resettled refugees in Atlanta, Georgia. One family that made a particular impact on me came from Zaire (now the Congo). In September of 1991, the father in the family preached a sermon denouncing injustice and corruption in his homeland. He used Gospel passages to speak out against oppression and human rights abuse, daring to challenge the dictator Mobutu Sese Seko. The night of his sermon, this minister's brother-in-law came to his house to warn him that his name had been placed on a hit list. The minister and his wife, who was a nurse, packed up their three sons—all under age six—and fled across the border into Uganda and then through Uganda to Kenya. There, they lived in a refugee camp where there was never sufficient food or water, where the family of five shared one tent, where they were never able to secure their personhood or belongings. They lived in this state of insecurity and fear until March of 1993 when they were granted refugee status and arrived in the United States.

A few years later, they had built a new life thanks to their own considerable strength and the generosity of a local United Methodist Church, and I had left this work to pursue graduate studies at Vanderbilt University. In a class during my first semester, Hebrew Bible Professor Renita Weems asked us to interview someone about his or her experience with suffering. I went back to Atlanta to meet with this family and spend some time talking with the father/husband. I was prepared to hear about his struggles with despair, his sense of abandonment, his rage against God. What I heard instead was an unshakeable faith, a persistent and completely unreasonable belief in God's unfailing presence and even God's loving care. Out of my own precocious cynicism and sheer incomprehension, I pressed him on this. Didn't you feel angry, abandoned, despairing? No, he replied, with such a beautiful sincerity that it only made me more confused.

That conversation had a profound effect on me. And every time that I hear someone who seems to have no reasonable cause for hope declare it, I am reminded of the confusion and humility I felt sitting in this family's living room. I continue to believe that we who have the time, space, and support to reflect and write about hope must be accountable to all of the legitimate reasons for despair and anger. But we who have the luxury of reflecting on hope and on the possibility of living without it must also remain accountable to those expressions of utterly unreasonable faith. That is, sometimes saying something meaningful to those in desperate situations means being quiet and listening to their grief, rage, and hope. Listening with compassion is a practice of hope.

Being accountable to those who suffer also requires that we who have the strength, support, and resources to intentionally cultivate a habit of hope must do so. As Sharon Welch insists, we must not fall to "cultured despair." As she explains, "cultured despair is marked by two distinct features: (1) the despair is cultured in the sense of its erudite awareness of the extent and complexity of many forms of injustice; and (2) the knowledge of the extent of injustice is accompanied by despair, in the sense of being unable to act in defiance of that injustice."[5] One underlying factor here is the assumption "that it is possible to guarantee the efficacy of one's actions," and that when such a guarantee cannot be attained, one should not act.[6] One perceives that there is nothing to be done, primarily because one cannot guarantee the outcome of any one act.

In order to find a source of hope and a cause for agency, then, Welch turns to people whose life experience has not frequently provided them a sense of control. She draws on the theological scholarship and fiction of African American women to identify practices of solidarity and accountability that comprise an ethic of risk. She captures the spirit of this ethic by contrasting it to Reinhold Niebuhr's Serenity Prayer, "God grant me the courage to change what I can, the serenity to accept what I cannot change, and the wisdom to know the difference." She comments, "The drive of the moral life is that we can never know the difference between that which we can change and that which we cannot. Our challenge is to move creatively in a very different sort of adventure, one whose prayer is more like this: 'What improbable task, with which unpredictable results, shall we undertake today?'"[7] Hope that is rooted in relational concepts of power requires this posture of prayer, namely one that does not assume that we can guarantee the efficacy of our action, nor that we should rely on the unidirectional power of a commander-in-chief. That is, we have both more responsibility and less assurance in this system.

One way to cultivate hope in this context is to practice the "politics of prefiguration." In her book *Hope in the Dark*, activist-writer Rebecca Solnit demonstrates this practice by telling stories of hope mined from current peace and social justice movements. Her examples (at least for those of us who share her vision for a peaceful and just world) constitute a seed-like presence of that which is hoped for. This seed-like presence becomes not only a source of hope, encouraging us by increasing our sense of possibility, it also becomes a place in which to live out the vision itself. Like the activists in El Salvador, one creates space for freedom. "Politics of prefiguration" means that "if you embody what you aspire to you have already succeeded. That is to say if your activism is already democratic, peaceful, creative, then in one small corner of the world these things have triumphed. Activism, in this model, is not only a toolbox to change things but a home in which to take up residence and live according to your beliefs—even if it's a temporary and local place."[8]

Another practice of hope, related to this, is to choose to believe in the preposterous assertion of beauty amidst tragedy. The writer Barbara Kingsolver demonstrates this practice in her book *Small Wonder*. The first essay in this book tells the story of a family in Afghanistan whose child wanders off and miraculously (or naturally, as Kingsolver asserts) finds refuge with a bear that nourishes and protects him. It is such a powerful story because Kingsolver describes the anguish of the family and because she places this small wonder in its context among other events in the fall of 2001, the terrorist attacks in the United States and the subsequent bombing of Afghanistan. She remains accountable to the cycle of violence, hatred, and fear surrounding her *and* she chooses to believe this small wonder. She explains,

> You could read this story and declare 'impossible,' even though many witnesses have sworn it's true. Or you could read this story and think of how warm lives are drawn to one another in cold places, think of the unconquerable force of a mother's love, the fact of the DNA code that we share in its great majority with other mammals—you could think of all that and say, Of course the bear nursed the baby. He was crying from hunger, she had milk. Small wonder.[9]

Embedded in tragic stories, one sometimes finds moments of beauty. These moments do not redeem the tragedy or justify it in any way whatsoever. But they do, sometimes, enable one to survive it. To paraphrase Wendy Farley in *Tragic Vision and Divine Compassion*, they provide strength for resisting suffering and for resisting the power that suffering has on its victims.

Sometimes we practice hope by doing everything we can to unearth a moment of beauty and then to defend it vigorously from all that threatens to push it back underground. If that moment of beauty is an act of unexpected generosity, we fight off the voices of perfectionist cynicism that remind us how far it falls from addressing structural injustice. Yes, we must address structural injustice, but we can also celebrate an act of generosity. As Rebecca Solnit advises us, we must not allow perfection to be "a stick with which to beat the possible." [10] If that moment of beauty is a friendship that develops as two people struggle for change that does not come, then we must do everything we can to preserve that friendship rather than allowing it to become another victim of a political defeat. Sometimes the object of hope is not so much something we strive toward as something that we vigorously defend each and every day.

Sometimes this defense assumes the form of stubborn insistence on hope itself though the evidence for it is hidden, dimly perceived, or barely there. At the start of the 2005 school year, I was invited to offer a story as part of morning prayer on a day devoted to the theme of social engagement. I prepared some stories that I could describe and offer as sources of hope for those who feel called to engage a violent and difficult world. But I ended up telling another story altogether, one supplied to me by my daughter, Katherine.

The week of this event, Katherine's body was having an all-too-frequent bout with a virus that typically put her through three days and nights of high fever and then two days of rash. On the third night, she woke up around 1:00 in the morning with a low-grade fever and raring to go. She spent most of the next two hours practicing her new words and activities in her crib while I lay on the floor alternately loving the sounds and longing for silence. Her new word was "hop" with a corresponding, awkward, uneven-legged, airborne millisecond. After working on this quite a while, she figured out something else. Over the last week, she had begun announcing her bowel movements with a pat on her diaper and the phrase, "I poo-poo." In the wee hours of this morning, she added that personal pronoun to her word-action to declare, "I HOP! I HOP! I HOP!" This additional word gave her such momentum that she continued to practice it until nearly 3:00 a.m. when she finally went back to sleep.

As I drove to school the next morning, feeling jittery from insufficient sleep and excessive compensation coffee, I rehearsed the stories I had planned to tell while Katherine rode along in the backseat. Then, I reached my main point: "So, these stories serve as *sources of hope* for me." From the backseat came the refrain, "I HOP! I HOP! I HOP!" I laughed so hard I cried.

Sometimes, Katherine's practice is the practice we need. In the face of all obstacles and barriers, and even in the wake of defeat, we need to declare, "I HOPE! I HOPE! I HOPE!" In these moments, this stubborn declaration is required to survive. And jumping along with it wouldn't hurt, even if this corresponding action is awkward, uneven, and brief. Indeed, another reason to insist on the *practice* of hope is to affirm our ability to cultivate it actively and intentionally. Hope is not a barometer responding passively to the influences of daily life. We can—and do— unearth cause to hope. In Kingsolver's words, we can "learn to be in love with...life again."[11] We stubbornly insist on the possibility of that which is unreasonable and irrational and outrageous, and we hold on to life and friendship amidst defeat.

Conclusion

In these days of striving and defending, we make mistakes. Our expectations rise too high or not high enough. We misdirect them completely, or just slightly. We do not gather the information necessary to ensure that our hope is appropriate and our assessment of its impediments accurate. And sometimes, we focus on the object of hope to the exclusion of the process by which it must be realized, and we harm the very thing we most want to embrace. We make mistakes not only in the object and amount of hope but also in its source. We place trust where we should not have or we sally forth alone without the support of friends. We declare human nature to be utterly flawed, and we give up on one another. We determine that God is either absent or cruel, and we give up on the Divine. I continue to speak of hope as a virtue not because I believe that Christian faith requires our acceptance of this divinely infused quality, but because life requires that we cultivate this habit that keeps us attentive to promise and peril.

Hope must be practiced because it is essential to daily life, the moral life, and the Christian life and because responsible hope does not come naturally. We must practice hope in order to cultivate it as a disposition. And, given the often overwhelming experiences of life, we must frequently practice hope in pieces, sometimes grieving and shouting, sometimes celebrating. The cumulative effect of such practices is a disposition that generates and sustains moral action because it attends to possibilities and to limitations. It buoys the spirit and steels the spine.

One last practice of hope already has a place in the liturgical calendar. On All Saints' Day, we do exactly what this book commends. We remember the dead by reading aloud their names and by calling into presence the countless others whose names we do not know. This is a spiritual practice that keeps us attentive to tragedy because we mourn the loss of these people and rage against a world that caused them to suffer. This is also a spiritual practice that keeps us accountable to possibility, for we also remember the dead by celebrating their lives. We give thanks for their enduring influence on us; we recall the dignity with which they resisted suffering, whether or not they triumphed over it; we rededicate ourselves to the causes they served and the relationships they valued. We sing, "For All the Saints":

> O blest communion, fellowship divine!
> We feebly struggle, they in glory shine;
> Yet all are one in thee, for all are thine.
> Alleluia, Alleluia!
>
> And when the strife is fierce, the warfare long,
> Steals on the ear the distant triumph song,
> And hearts are brave again, and arms are strong.
> Alleluia, Alleluia![12]

This most powerful hymn has the potential to become an irresponsible expression of triumphalism if we extract it from its context of somber remembrance. Likewise, reading the names of the dead has the potential to become an irresponsible expression of despair if we extract it from its context of gratitude and rededication. All Saints' Day exemplifies the disposition of responsible hope. It is a day that holds us accountable to possibility and limitation, cultivating hope through promise and peril.

Select Bibliography

Aertsen, Jan. "Aquinas's Philosophy in its Historical Setting." In *The Cambridge Companion to Aquinas*, ed. Norman Krezman and Eleonore Stump. New York: Cambridge University Press, 1993.

Aquinas, Saint Thomas. *Questiones Disputatae de Potentia Dei*. Translated by the English Dominican Fathers. Westminster, Md.: Newman Press, 1932. Reprint 1952.

———. *Summa Theologiae*. Second and revised edition, 1920. Translated by Fathers of the English Dominican Province. Online edition 2003 by Kevin Knight.

———. *Treatise on the Virtues*. Translated by John A. Oesterle. Notre Dame: University of Notre Dame Press, 1966.

Aristotle. *Nicomachean Ethics*. Translated with introduction and notes by Martin Ostwald. Englewood Cliffs, N.J.: Prentice Hall, 1962.

Augustine. *Concerning the City of God against the Pagans*. Translated by Henry Bettenson. London: Penguin Books, 1972. Reprint, with an introduction by John O'Meara, 1984.

———. *The Confessions of St. Augustine*. Translated by Rex Warner. New York: Penguin, 1963.

———. *Enchiridion*. In *Ancient Christian Writers*. Translated by Louis A. Arand, S.S. Westminster, Md.: Newman Press, 1963.

———. *On Free Choice of the Will*. Translated by Anna S. Benjamin and L. H. Hackstaff, with an introduction by L. H. Hackstaff. Macmillan Library of Liberal Arts. New York: Macmillan, 1964.

Beasley-Murray, G. R. *Jesus and the Kingdom of God*. Grand Rapids: Eerdmans, 1986.

Beckley, Harlan. *Passion for Justice: Retrieving the Legacies of Walter Rauschenbusch, John A. Ryan, and Reinhold Niebuhr*. Louisville: Westminster/John Knox Press, 1992.

Blount, Brian K. *Go Preach! Mark's Kingdom Message and the Black Church Today*. Maryknoll: Orbis, 1998.

Braaten, Carl E. *Eschatology and Ethics: Essays on the Theology and Ethics of the Kingdom of God*. Minneapolis: Augsburg, 1974.

———. "The Kingdom of God and Life Everlasting." In *Christian Theology: An Introduction to Its Traditions and Tasks*, ed. Peter C. Hodgson and Robert H. King, 328-52. Minneapolis: Fortress Press, 1994.

Cahill, Lisa Sowle. "Consent in Time of Affliction: The Ethics of a Circumspect Theist." *Journal of Religious Ethics* 13 (Spring 1985): 22-36.

Case-Winters, Anna. *God's Power: Traditional Understandings and Contemporary Challenges*. Louisville: Westminster/John Knox Press, 1990.

Chilton, Bruce. *Pure Kingdom: Jesus' Vision of God*. Grand Rapids: Eerdmans, 1996.

Chopp, Rebecca S., and Mark Lewis Taylor. "Introduction: Crisis, Hope, and Contemporary Theology." In *Reconstructing Christian Theology*, ed. Chopp and Taylor, 1-24. Minneapolis: Fortress Press, 1994.

Clark, Henry. *Serenity, Courage, and Wisdom: The Enduring Legacy of Reinhold Niebuhr*. Cleveland: Pilgrim Press, 1994.

Cone, James. *A Black Theology of Liberation*, 2d ed. Maryknoll: Orbis Books, 1986.

———. *Black Theology and Black Power*. New York: Seabury Press, 1969.

Crawford, A. Elaine Brown. *Hope in the Holler: A Womanist Theology*. Louisville: Westminster/John Knox Press, 2002.

Evans Jr., James H. *We Have Been Believers: An African-American Systematic Theology*. Minneapolis: Fortress Press, 1992.

Farley, Wendy. *Tragic Vision and Divine Compassion: A Contemporary Theodicy*. Louisville: Westminster/John Knox Press, 1990.

Fowler, James W. *To See the Kingdom: The Theological Vision of H. Richard Niebuhr*. Nashville: Abingdon Press, 1974. Reprint, Eugene, Ore.: Wipf & Stock, 2001.

Fox, Richard Wightman. *Reinhold Niebuhr: A Biography.* New York: Pantheon Books, 1985; Ithaca, N.Y.: Cornell University Press, 1996.

Gustafson, James M. *Can Ethics Be Christian?* Chicago: University of Chicago Press, 1975.

————. *Christ and the Moral Life.* Chicago: University of Chicago Press, 1968.

————. *Ethics from a Theocentric Perspective.* Vol. 1, *Theology and Ethics.* Chicago: University of Chicago Press, 1981.

————. *Ethics from a Theocentric Perspective.* Vol. 2, *Ethics and Theology.* Chicago: University of Chicago Press, 1984.

————. "A Response to Critics." *Journal of Religious Ethics* 13 (Fall, 1985): 185-209.

Gutiérrez, Gustavo. *A Theology of Liberation: History, Politics and Salvation: Revised Edition with a New Introduction.* Translated and edited by Sister Caridad Inda and John Eagleson. Maryknoll: Orbis Books, 1988.

Harnack, Adolf von. *What Is Christianity.* Translated by Thomas Bailey Saunders. San Francisco: Harper & Brothers, 1957. Fortress Texts in Modern Theology. Philadelphia: Fortress Press, 1986.

Hartt, Julian. "Encounter and Inference in Our Awareness of God." In *The God Experience: Essays in Hope,* ed. Joseph P. Whelan, S.J. New York: Newman Press, 1971.

Hodgson, Peter C. *God in History: Shapes of Freedom.* Nashville: Abingdon Press, 1989.

————. *Winds of the Spirit: A Constructive Christian Theology.* Louisville: Westminster/John Knox Press, 1994.

Horsley, Richard A. *Jesus and Empire: The Kingdom of God and the New World Disorder.* Minneapolis: Fortress Press, 2003.

Humphries, Michael L. *Christian Origins and the Language of the Kingdom of God.* Carbondale, Ill.: Southern Illinois University Press, 1999.

Johnson, Elizabeth. *Friends of God and Prophets: A Feminist Theological Reading of the Communion of Saints.* New York: Continuum, 1998.

————. *She Who Is: The Mystery of God in Feminist Discourse.* New York: Crossroad, 1992.

————. *Women, Earth, and Creator Spirit*. 1993 Madeleva Lecture in Spirituality. New York: Paulist Press, 1993.

Kaylor, David R. *Jesus the Prophet: His Vision of the Kingdom on Earth*. Louisville: Westminster/John Knox Press, 1994.

Keller, Catherine. *Apocalypse Now and Then*. Boston: Beacon Press, 1996.

————. "Eschatology, Ecology, and a Green Ecumenacy." In *Reconstructing Christian Theology*, ed. Rebecca S. Chopp and Mark Lewis Taylor, 326-45. Minneapolis: Fortress Press, 1994.

————. "Pneumatic Nudges: The Theology of Moltmann, Feminism, and the Future." In *The Future of Theology: Essays in Honor of Jürgen Moltmann*, ed. Miroslav Volf, Carmen Krieg, and Thomas Kucharz, 142-53. Grand Rapids: William B. Eerdmans Publishing Co., 1996.

Kenny, Anthony. *The God of the Philosophers*. Oxford: Clarendon, 1979.

Kingsolver, Barbara. *High Tide: Essays from Now or Never*. New York: HarperCollins, 1995.

————. *Small Wonder: Essays*. New York: Perennial HarperCollins, 2002.

Lane, Dermot. *Keeping Hope Alive: Stirrings in Christian Theology*. New York: Paulist Press, 1996.

Le Masters, Philip. *Discipleship for All Believers: Christian Ethics and the Kingdom of God*. Scottdale, Penn.: Herald Press, 1992.

Lovin, Robin. *Reinhold Niebuhr and Christian Realism*. New York: Cambridge University Press, 1995.

Lynch, William F. *Images of Hope: Imagination as Healer of the Hopeless*. Notre Dame: University of Notre Dame Press, 1965.

Malina, Bruce J. *The Social Gospel of Jesus: The Kingdom of God in Mediterranean Perspective*. Minneapolis: Fortress Press, 2001.

McCann, Dennis. *Christian Realism and Liberation Theology: Practical Theologies in Creative Conflict*. Maryknoll: Orbis Books, 1981.

McFague, Sallie. *The Body of God: An Ecological Theology*. Minneapolis: Fortress Press, 1993.

————. "Human Beings, Embodiment, and Our Home the Earth." In *Reconstructing Christian Theology*, ed. Rebecca Chopp and Mark Lewis Taylor, 141-69. Minneapolis: Fortress Press, 1994.

————. *Super, Natural Christians: How We Should Love Nature.* Minneapolis: Fortress Press, 1997.

McManus, Philip. "Argentina's Mothers of Courage." In *Relentless Persistence: Nonviolent Action in Latin America*, ed. Philip McManus and Gerald Schlabach, 79-99. Philadelphia: New Society Publishers, 1991.

Metz, Johann Baptist. *Faith in History & Society: Toward a Practical Fundamental Theology.* New York: Seabury Press, 1980.

Minus, Paul M. *Walter Rauschenbusch: An American Reformer.* New York: Macmillan, 1988.

Mitchell, Lynn E. *The Vision of the New Community: Public Ethics in the Light of Christian Eschatology.* New York: Peter Lang, 1988.

Moltmann, Jürgen. "An Autobiographical Note." Translated by Charles White. In *God, Hope, and History: Jürgen Moltmann and the Christian Concept of History*, ed. A. J. Conyers, 203-23. Macon: Mercer University Press, 1988.

————. *The Coming of God: Christian Eschatology.* Translated by Margaret Kohl. Minneapolis: Fortress Press, 1996.

————. *The Crucified God: The Cross of Christ as the Foundation and Criticism of Christian Theology.* Translated by R.A. Wilson and John Bowden. San Francisco: HarperCollins, 1974.

————. *God in Creation: A New Theology of Creation and the Spirit of God.* Translated by Margaret Kohl. San Francisco: Harper San Francisco, 1991.

————. *On Human Dignity: Political Theology and Ethics.* Translated by M. Douglas Meeks. Philadelphia: Fortress Press, 1984.

————. *Religion, Revolution and the Future.* Translated by M. Douglas Meeks. New York: Charles Scribner's Sons, 1969.

————. *The Spirit of Life: A Universal Affirmation.* Translated by Margaret Kohl. Minneapolis: Fortress Press, 1992.

————. *Theology of Hope: On the Ground and the Implications of a Christian Eschatology.* Translated by James W. Leitch. New York: Harper & Row, 1967.

————. *The Trinity and the Kingdom: The Doctrine of God.* Translated by Margaret Kohl. San Francisco: Harper & Row, 1981.

Moore Robinson, Margaret Anne. "Moving Beyond Symbol and Myth:

Understanding the Kingdom of God through Metaphor." Ph.D. diss., Claremont Graduate University, 2004.

Niebuhr, H. Richard. *Faith on Earth: An Inquiry into the Structure of Human Faith.* New Haven: Yale University Press, 1989.

———. *The Kingdom of God in America.* New York: Harper & Row, 1937.

———. *Radical Monotheism and Western Culture: With Supplementary Essays.* With a foreword by James Gustafson. New York: Harper, 1960. Reprint, Louisville: Westminster/John Knox, 1993.

———. *The Responsible Self: An Essay in Christian Moral Philosophy.* San Francisco: Harper & Row, 1963.

———. *Theology, History and Culture,* ed. William Stacy Johnson. New Haven: Yale University Press, 1996.

Niebuhr, Reinhold. *An Interpretation of Christian Ethics.* San Francisco: Harper & Brothers, 1935. Reprint, San Francisco: Harper & Row, 1963.

———. *Christian Realism and Political Problems.* New York: Charles Scribner's Sons, 1953.

———. *Moral Man and Immoral Society: A Study in Ethics and Politics.* New York: Charles Scribner's Sons, 1932. First Touchstone Edition, New York: Simon & Schuster, 1995.

———. *The Nature and Destiny of Man.* Vol. 1, *Human Nature.* New York: Charles Scribner's Sons, 1941, 1964.

———. *The Nature and Destiny of Man.* Vol. 2, *Human Destiny.* New York: Charles Scribner's Sons, 1943, 1964.

Pannenberg, Wolfhart. *Theology and the Kingdom of God.* Philadelphia: Westminster Press, 1969.

Perrin, Norman. *Jesus and the Language of the Kingdom: Symbol and Metaphor in New Testament Interpretation.* Philadephia: Fortress Press, 1976.

Pieper, Josef. *Faith, Hope, Love.* San Francisco: Ignatius Press, 1997.

Rauschenbusch, Walter. *A Theology for the Social Gospel.* New York: Macmillan, 1917. Reprint, Nashville: Abingdon Press, 1990.

———. *Christianity and the Social Crisis.* New York: Macmillan, 1907. Reprint, Louisville: Westminster/John Knox Press, 1991.

————. *Christianizing the Social Order*. New York: Macmillan Co., 1912.

————. *Selected Writings*, ed. Winthrop Hudson. New York: Paulist Press, 1984.

Ringe, Sharon. "Solidarity and Contextuality: Readings of Matthew 18:21-35." In *Reading from This Place: Social Location and Biblical Interpretation*, ed. Fernando Segovia and Mary Ann Tolbert, Vol 1. Minneapolis: Fortress Press, 1994.

Ringe, Sharon H. and H. C. Paul Kim, eds. *Literary Encounters with the Reign of God*. New York: T&T Clark International, 2004.

Ross, Sir David. *Aristotle*, 6th ed. London: Routledge, 1995.

Ruether, Rosemary Radford. "Eschatology and Feminism." In *Lift Every Voice: Constructive Christian Theologies from the Underside*, ed. Susan Brooks Thistlethwaite and Mary Potter Engel, 129-42. San Francisco: Harper & Row, 1990.

————. *Sexism and God-Talk: Toward a Feminist Theology: With a New Introduction*. Boston: Beacon Press, 1993.

Sands, Kathleen M. *Escape from Paradise: Evil and Tragedy in Feminist Theology*. Minneapolis: Fortress Press, 1994.

Segovia, Fernando and Mary Ann Tolbert, eds. *Reading from This Place: Social Location and Biblical Interpretation*. Vol. 1. Minneapolis: Fortress Press, 1994.

Solnit, Rebecca. *Hope in the Dark: Untold Stories, Wild Possibilities*. New York: Nation Books, 2004.

Suchocki, Marjorie Hewitt. *The Fall to Violence: Original Sin in Relational Theology*. New York: Continuum, 1995.

————. *God, Christ, Church: A Practical Guide to Process Theology*. New York: Crossroad, 1995.

Thistlethwaite, Susan Brooks and Peter C. Hodgson. "The Church, Classism, and Ecclesial Community." In *Reconstructing Christian Theology*, ed. Rebecca S. Chopp and Mark Lewis Taylor, 303-25. Minneapolis: Fortress Press, 1994.

Tillich, Paul. "The Right to Hope: A Sermon." In *Paul Tillich: Theologian of the Boundaries*, ed. Mark Kline Taylor, 324-31. Minneapolis: Fortress Press, 1991.

Townes, Emilie. *Embracing the Spirit: Womanist Perspectives on Hope, Salvation and Transformation*. Maryknoll: Orbis Books, 1997.

Troeltsch, Ernst. *The Christian Faith*. Translated by Garrett E. Paul. Fortress Texts in Modern Theology. Minneapolis: Fortress Press, 1991.

————. *Christian Thought: Its History and Application: Lectures Written for Delivery in England during March 1923*, ed. Baron F. von Hügel. Westport, Conn.: Hyperion Press, 1979.

————. *Ernst Troeltsch: Writings on Theology and Religion*. Edited and translated by Robert Morgan and Michael Pye. Louisville: Westminster/John Knox Press, 1977.

————. *Religion in History*. Translated by James Luther Adams and Walter F. Bense. Minneapolis: Fortress Press, 1991.

————. *The Social Teaching of the Christian Churches*. 2 vols. Translated by Olive Wyon. London: George Allen & Unwin Ltd., 1931. Reprint, Library of Theological Ethics. Louisville: Westminster/John Knox Press, 1992.

The United Methodist Hymnal: Book of United Methodist Worship. Nashville: United Methodist Publishing House, 1989.

Welch, Claude. *Protestant Thought in the Nineteenth Century*. 2 vols. New Haven: Yale University Press, 1972-1985.

Welch, Sharon. *A Feminist Ethic of Risk*. Minneapolis: Fortress Press, 1990.

Yoder, John Howard. *The Politics of Jesus*. Grand Rapids: William Eerdmans Publishing Group, 1972.

Notes

Introduction

1. Philip McManus and Gerald Schlabach, eds., *Relentless Persistence: Nonviolent Action in Latin America* (Philadelphia: New Society Publishers, 1991).

2. I learned the practice of "calling into presence" from Molly Graver, who taught me about gatherings in El Salvador that would begin by calling into presence those martyred and disappeared in the struggle.

3. Stephen A. Nash, Robert Rosenblum, Brigitte Baer, eds., *Picasso and the War Years: 1937-1945* (London: Thames & Hudson, 1998).

Chapter 1: The Problem of Hope

1. Hab. 1:2-3 NRSV.

2. Judith E. Sanderson, "Habakkuk," in *Women's Bible Commentary*, ed. Carol A. Newsom and Sharon H. Ringe (Louisville: Westminster/John Knox Press, 1998), 237. See also Robert D. Haak, *Habakkuk* (Leiden: E.J. Brill, 1992), 114.

3. Hab. 1:6, 9 RSV.

4. Hab. 1:9 RSV.

5. Hab. 1:10 RSV.

6. Hab. 1:13 RSV.

7. Sanderson, "Habakkuk," 238.

8. Hab. 3:9-13 RSV.

9. Hab. 3:13 RSV.

10. Hab. 3:16 NRSV.

11. Hab. 3:17-19 NRSV.

12. Sanderson, "Habakkuk," 237. Sanderson also provides a helpful commentary on the "prevalence of violence and the image of the divine warrior-king" in this text (238-239).

13. Hab. 3:18 NRSV.

14. Jer. 6:14.

15. I owe this language of "shadow side" to Carol Lakey Hess.

16. Jürgen Moltmann, *Theology of Hope: On the Ground and the Implications of a Christian Eschatology*, trans. James W. Leitch (New York: Harper & Row, 1967), 16.

17. William F. Lynch, *Images of Hope: Imagination as Healer of the Hopeless* (Notre Dame: University of Notre Dame Press, 1965), 32.

18. Lynch, *Images of Hope*, 23.

19. Lynch, *Images of Hope*, 36.

20. Moltmann, *Theology of Hope*, 21.

21. Paul Tillich, "The Right to Hope: A Sermon" in *Paul Tillich: Theologian on the Boundaries*, ed. Mark Kline Taylor (Minneapolis: Fortress Press, 1991), 325.

22. Dermot Lane, *Keeping Hope Alive: Stirrings in Christian Theology* (New York: Paulist Press, 1996), 60.

23. I use John A. Oesterle's translation of Saint Thomas Aquinas's *Treatise on the Virtues* for questions 49-67 of the *Summa Theologiae* (Notre Dame: University of Notre Dame Press, 1984), I-II.62.4.

24. Aquinas, *Treatise*, I-II.62.3.

25. The *basileia tou theou* is most often translated as the kingdom of God. However, twentieth-century theologians propose several English alternatives in order to avoid hierarchical and masculine imagery. These issues of interpretation will be addressed in subsequent pages. In the meantime, I will use the Greek unless I am presenting a particular person's view of this faith claim.

26. I am drawing on the Latin word *religare* from which we derive our word "religion." *Religare* suggests something that is binding or that which constrains. I am also drawing on a distinction made by James M. Gustafson (and others) between belief and faith, whereby the latter is understood to denote a more personal and perhaps deeper commitment on the part of an individual. See James

M. Gustafson, *Can Ethics Be Christian?* (Chicago: University of Chicago Press, 1975), 48.

27. James M. Gustafson, *Can Ethics Be Christian?*, 66. Gustafson refers to Julian Hartt's essay, "Encounter and Inference in Our Awareness of God," in *The God Experience: Essays in Hope*, ed. Joseph P. Whelan, S.J. (New York: Newman Press, 1971), 49.

28. Gustafson, *Can Ethics Be Christian?*, 54.

29. See Ernst Troeltsch, "The Historical and Dogmatic Method in Theology" in *Religion in History*, trans. James Luther Adams (Minneapolis: Fortress, 1991); "What Does 'Essence of Christianity' Mean?" in *Writings on Theology and Religion*, trans. and ed. Robert Morgan and Michael Pye (Louisville: Westminster John Knox, 1977). See also Claude Welch, "Ernst Troeltsch: Faith, History, and Ethics in Tension" in *Protestant Thought in the Nineteenth Century*, vol. 2. (New Haven: Yale University Press, 1985); Ernst Troeltsch, *The Social Teaching of the Christian Churches*, trans. Olive Wyon (London: George Allen & Unwin Ltd., 1931; repr., Library of Theological Ethics. Louisville: Westminster/John Knox Press, 1992), 999-1000 (page citations are to reprint edition).

30. H. Richard Niebuhr, *Christ and Culture* (New York: Harper & Row, 1951). H. Richard Niebuhr, *The Kingdom of God in America*, First Harper Torchbook Edition (New York: Harper & Row, 1937; 1959). In several posthumously published lectures, Niebuhr explained his understanding of the relationship between faith, history, and ethics more fully. See H. Richard Niebuhr, *Theology, History and Culture*, ed. William Stacy Johnson (New Haven: Yale University Press, 1996).

31. This translation of the *basileia* is used by Sharon H. Ringe and was brought to my attention by Peter C. Hodgson. For discussion of it, see Ringe's essay, "Solidarity and Contextuality: Readings of Matthew 18:21-35," in *Reading from This Place: Social Location and Biblical Interpretation*, vol. 1, ed. Fernando Segovia and Mary Ann Tolbert (Minneapolis: Fortress Press, 1994).

32. James Gustafson, "A Response to Critics," *Journal of Religious Ethics* 13 (Fall 1985): 185.

33. There are also important arguments for utopian ethics. See, for example,

Ada María Isasi-Díaz, *La Lucha Continues: Mujerista Theology* (Maryknoll: Orbis, 2004), 164-69.

Chapter 2: A History of Hope

1. Jan Aertsen, "Aquinas's Philosophy in its Historical Setting," in *The Cambridge Companion to Aquinas*, ed. Norman Krezman and Eleonore Stump (New York: Cambridge University Press, 1993), 12.

2. See Aertsen, "Aquinas's Philosophy in its Historical Setting," 14-20.

3. Saint Thomas Aquinas, *Summa Theologiae*, I-II.40.2.

4. Aquinas, *ST*, I-II.40.1. These first two characteristics reflect Augustine's teaching in *The Enchiridion* (chapter 2.8). By contrast to faith, which pertains to past, present, and future and may be placed in evil or good, hope "deals only with things that are good and which lie only in the future." Augustine, *Enchiridion*, in *Ancient Christian Writers*, trans. Louis A. Arand, S.S. (Westminster, Md.: Newman Press, 1963).

5. Aquinas, *ST*, I-II.40.1.

6. Aquinas, *ST*, I-II.40.5.

7. Aquinas, *ST*, I-II.40.2.

8. Aquinas, *ST*, I-II.40.2.

9. Aquinas, *ST*, I-II.40.5.

10. Aquinas, *ST*, I-II.40.5.

11. Aquinas, *ST*, I-II.40.5.

12. I should note that this point comes from Aristotle's discussion of optimism as something similar to but less than courage (in *Nicomachean Ethics*, Book III, Article 8). Aristotle is critical of the optimist who assumes that past success demonstrates invincibility. To be true to Aristotle's point, therefore, one should amend Aquinas thusly: experience causes hope in the first sense when it "enhance[s] a man's [belief in his] ability." The courageous man would be more realistic about ability; the optimist is overly confident about ability. This important distinction will be discussed in more detail later in this chapter.

13. Aquinas, *ST*, I-II.40.5.

14. Of course, one must question the subjective element of this determination.

In his commentary on this point, Josef Pieper suggests that a natural hope can be for something objectively bad. That is, I may hope for something that is good only for me, but bad for everyone else. However, Pieper goes on to argue, hope as a theological virtue can only be for something objectively good (100). As we will see, Aquinas identifies the object of the theological virtue of hope to be God, though there may also be some other objects of hope that are instrumental to this final one. See Pieper, *Faith, Hope, Love* (San Francisco: Ignatius Press, 1997).

15. Aristotle, *Nicomachean Ethics*, translated with an introduction and notes by Martin Ostwald (Englewood Cliffs, N.J.: Prentice Hall, 1962), xii. Also see Sir David Ross, *Aristotle*, 6th ed. (London: Routledge, 1995), 16.

16. Aertsen, "Aquinas's Philosophy in its Historical Setting," 20.

17. Aristotle, *Nicomachean Ethics*, 1.13.1103a.10.

18. Aristotle, *Nicomachean Ethics*, 1.7.1097a.30.

19. Aristotle, *Nicomachean Ethics*, 1.7.1097b.20.

20. Aristotle, *Nicomachean Ethics*, 1.7.1097b.20-25.

21. Martin Ostwald, Glossary to Aristotle's *Nicomachean Ethics* (Englewood Cliffs, N.J.: Prentice Hall, 1962), 308-9. Ostwald explains that *hexis* means "characteristic, also trained ability, characteristic condition, characteristic attitude. A noun related to the verb *echein*, 'to have,' 'hold,' 'hold as a possession,' 'be in a certain condition,' designating a firmly fixed possession of the mind, established by repeated and habitual action. Once attained, it is ever present, at least in a potential form. The Latin interpreters of Greek philosophy rendered the term by *habitus*, a word which well retains the original relation with *habēre=echein*. Hence 'habit' has often been used as an English equivalent" (308-9).

22. Aristotle, *Nicomachean Ethics*, 2.6.1106a.15-20.

23. Aristotle, *Nicomachean Ethics*, 2.1.1103a.15.

24. Aristotle, *Nicomachean Ethics*, 2.1.1103a.15-20.

25. Aristotle, *Nicomachean Ethics*, 2.1.1103a.25.

26. Aristotle, *Nicomachean Ethics*, 2.1.1103b.

27. Aristotle, *Nicomachean Ethics*, 2.2.1103b.30.

28. Augustine, *On Free Choice of the Will*, trans. Anna S. Benjamin and L. H. Hackstaff, with introduction by L. H. Hackstaff (New York: Macmillan, 1964), 2.19.

29. Augustine, *On Free Choice of the Will*, 2.19.

30. Augustine, *Concerning the City of God Against the Pagans*, trans. Henry Bettenson (London: Penguin, 1972; repr., with an introduction by John O'Meara, 1984), 19.4.

31. Augustine, *Concerning the City of God*, 19.1.

32. Augustine, *Concerning the City of God*, 14.26.

33. Saint Thomas Aquinas, *Treatise on the Virtues*, I-II.57.1.

34. Aquinas, *Treatise*, I-II.62.1.

35. Aquinas, *Treatise*, I-II.62.1.

36. Augustine, *Enchiridion*, 30.114-115.

37. Augustine, *Confessions*, trans. Rex Warner (New York: Penguin, 1963), x.29.

38. Aquinas, *Treatise*, I-II.67.4.

39. Aquinas, *Treatise*, I-II.62.4.

40. Aquinas, *Treatise*, I-II.64.4.

41. Aquinas, *Treatise*, I-II.64.4.

42. Aristotle, *Nicomachean Ethics*, 2.2.1104a.25.

43. Aristotle, *Nicomachean Ethics*, 2.9.1109b.5.

44. Aristotle, *Nicomachean Ethics*, 2.7.

45. Aristotle, *Nicomachean Ethics*, 3.7.1115b.5-20.

46. Aristotle, *Nicomachean Ethics*, 3.7.1115b.25.

47. Aristotle, *Nicomachean Ethics*, 3.7.1115b.35.

48. Aristotle, *Nicomachean Ethics*, 3.7.1116a.

49. Aquinas, *Treatise*, I-II.64.1-2.

50. Aquinas, *Treatise*, I-II.64.4.

51. Aquinas, *Treatise*, I-II.64.4.

52. Aquinas, *Treatise*, I-II.64.4, reply 3.

53. Aquinas, *ST*, II-II.17.4.

54. Aquinas, *ST*, II-II.17.4.

55. Aquinas, *ST*, II-II.17.4.

56. Aquinas, *ST*, II-II.17.5.

57. Aquinas, *ST*, II-II.17.5, objection 2.

58. Aquinas, *ST*, II-II.17.5, reply 2.

59. Aquinas, *ST*, II-II.17.5, reply 2.

60. I am indebted to Jean Porter for her suggestion that what is at issue here is really Aquinas's concept of omnipotence.

61. Saint Thomas Aquinas, *Questiones Disputatae de Potentia Dei* (On the Power of God), trans. English Dominican Fathers (Westminster, Md.: Newman Press, 1932; repr., 1952), 1.2 (11) (hereafter referred to as *DP*, page numbers in parentheses).

62. Aquinas, *DP*, 1.2 (11).

63. Aquinas, *DP*, 1.1 (4).

64. Anthony Kenny, *The God of the Philosophers* (Oxford: Clarendon Press, 1979), 97.

65. Aquinas, *DP*, 1.2 (12).

66. Aquinas, *DP*, 1.2 (12).

67. As this *disputatio* unfolds, Aquinas does note that this power may be limited by God's will and by reason (reply to objection 13, p. 14). Thus, Anthony Kenny describes Aquinas's definition of omnipotence as "the ability to do whatever is logically possible." However, Kenny also argues that Aquinas preferred the formulation of divine omnipotence as the infinite power of God (92). For further discussion of Aquinas's concept of omnipotence, see John F. Wippel, *Metaphysical Themes in Thomas Aquinas. Studies in the Philosophy and the History of Philosophy*, vol. 10. (Washington: Catholic University of America Press, 1984).

68. Aquinas, *DP*, 1.2, reply 1 (12).

69. Aquinas, *DP*, 1.2, reply 1 (12).

70. Aquinas, *DP*, 1.2, reply 1 (12).

71. Aquinas's assertion that God's power is manifested and known by its effects and his language of human beings as secondary efficient causes do provide a bridge of sorts. However, these proposals only provide support for the claim that God works through human beings as instruments, not that God works with human beings as co-laborers.

72. This language of hiding comes from Susan Nelson, whose article, "The Sin of Hiding: A Feminist Critique of Reinhold Niebuhr's Account of the Sin of

Pride," *Soundings* 65 (Fall 1982): 316-27, makes the feminist argument against an exclusive focus on the sin of pride.

73. See Anna Case-Winters, *God's Power: Traditional Understandings and Contemporary Challenges* (Louisville: Westminster/John Knox Press, 1990).

Chapter 3: Contemporary Voices of Hope

1. James Cone, *Black Theology and Black Power* (New York: Seabury Press, 1969), 123.

2. Paul Tillich, "The Right to Hope: A Sermon," in *Paul Tillich: Theologian on the Boundaries*, ed. Mark Kline Taylor (Minneapolis: Fortress Press, 1991), 327.

3. Jürgen Moltmann, *Theology of Hope: On the Ground and the Implications of a Christian Eschatology* (New York: Harper & Row, 1967), 179.

4. Walter Rauschenbusch, *Christianizing the Social Order* (New York: Macmillan Co., 1912), 6.

5. Rauschenbusch, *Christianizing the Social Order*, 5.

6. Reinhold Niebuhr, *An Interpretation of Christian Ethics* (San Francisco: Harper & Brothers, 1935; San Francisco: Harper & Row, 1963), 5.

7. Rauschenbusch, *Christianizing the Social Order*, 461-62.

8. Walter Rauschenbusch, "Social Motives in Evangelism," in *Selected Writings*, ed. Winthrop Hudson (New York: Paulist Press, 1984), 28-29.

9. Walter Rauschenbusch, *A Theology for the Social Gospel* (New York: Macmillan, 1917; Nashville: Abingdon Press, 1990), 226.

10. Rauschenbusch, *Christianizing the Social Order*, x.

11. Reinhold Niebuhr, *Moral Man and Immoral Society: A Study in Ethics and Politics* (New York: Charles Scribner's Sons, 1932; First Touchstone Edition, New York: Simon & Schuster, 1995), 81.

12. R. Niebuhr, *Moral Man and Immoral Society*, 81.

13. Reinhold Niebuhr, *An Interpretation of Christian Ethics* (San Francisco: Harper & Brothers, 1935; San Francisco: Harper & Row, 1963), 49.

14. Reinhold Niebuhr, *The Nature and Destiny of Man*, vol. 2, *Human Destiny* (New York: Charles Scribner's Sons, 1943, 1964), 207.

15. R. Niebuhr, *The Nature and Destiny of Man*, vol. 2, 207.

16. R. Niebuhr, *Moral Man and Immoral Society*, 22.

17. Sharon Welch, *A Feminist Ethic of Risk* (Minneapolis: Augsburg Fortress, 1989; rev. ed., 2000), 33.

18. Cone, *Black Theology and Black Power*, 123.

19. Jürgen Moltmann, *The Coming of God: Christian Eschatology* (Minneapolis: Fortress Press, 1996), 50.

20. Walter Rauschenbusch, "Our Attitude toward Millenarianism," in *Selected Writings*, ed. Winthrop Hudson (New York: Paulist Press, 1984), 90.

21. Elizabeth A. Johnson, *Friends of God and Prophets: A Feminist Theological Reading of the Communion of Saints* (New York: Continuum, 1998), 186.

22. Rosemary Radford Ruether, *Sexism and God-Talk: Toward a Feminist Theology*, with a new introduction (Boston: Beacon Press, 1993), 252.

23. Ruether, *Sexism and God-Talk*, 253.

24. Ruether, *Sexism and God-Talk*, 253.

25. Rauschenbusch, *A Theology for the Social Gospel*, 224.

26. Gustavo Gutiérrez, *A Theology of Liberation: History, Politics and Salvation Revised Edition with a New Introduction*. Trans. and ed. Sister Caridad Inda and John Eagleson (Maryknoll: Orbis Books, 1988), 97. Gutiérrez cites Isa. 65:21-22, Isa. 29:18-19, Matt. 11:5, Lev. 15:10 ff, Luke 4:16-21.

27. Ruether, *Sexism and God-Talk*, 232-33.

28. Moltmann, *Theology of Hope*, 18.

29. Moltmann, *Theology of Hope*, 21.

30. James Gustafson, "A Response to Critics," *Journal of Religious Ethics* 13 (Fall 1985): 198.

31. James Gustafson, *Ethics from a Theocentric Perspective*, vol. 1, *Ethics and Theology* (Chicago: University of Chicago Press, 1981), 18, 25.

32. Gustafson, *Ethics from a Theocentric Perspective*, vol. 1, 45.

33. Gustafson, *Ethics from a Theocentric Perspective*, vol. 1, 260.

34. Gustafson, *Ethics from a Theocentric Perspective*, vol. 1, 268.

35. Gustafson, *Ethics from a Theocentric Perspective*, vol. 1, 261.

36. Gustafson, *Ethics from a Theocentric Perspective*, vol 1, 164.

37. Gustafson, *Ethics from a Theocentric Perspective*, vol. 1, 167.

38. James Gustafson, *Ethics from a Theocentric Perspective*, vol. 2, *Ethics and Theology* (Chicago: University of Chicago Press, 1984), 22.

39. Lisa Sowle Cahill, "Consent in Time of Affliction: The Ethics of a Circumspect Theist," *Journal of Religious Ethics* 13 (Spring 1985): 24-25. Cahill is paraphrasing Gustafson's remarks here.

40. H. Richard Niebuhr, "Reflections on the Christian Theory of History," in *Theology, History and Culture*, ed. William Stacy Johnson (New Haven: Yale University Press, 1996), 85.

41. Walter Rauschenbusch, *Christianity and the Social Crisis* (New York: Macmillan, 1907; repr., Louisville: Wesminster/John Knox Press, 1991), 90, 94.

42. Rauschenbusch, *A Theology for the Social Gospel*, 225.

43. Jürgen Moltmann, *Religion, Revolution and the Future* (New York: Charles Scribner's Sons, 1969), 52-53.

44. Marjorie Hewitt Suchocki, *God, Christ, Church: A Practical Guide to Process Theology* (New York: Crossroad, 1995), 188-89.

45. Suchocki, *God, Christ, Church*, 190.

46. Suchocki, *God, Christ, Church*, 191.

47. Rosemary Radford Ruether, "Eschatology and Feminism," in *Lift Every Voice: Constructive Christian Theologies from the Underside*, ed. Susan Brooks Thistlethwaite and Mary Potter Engel (San Francisco: Harper & Row, 1990), 139.

48. Ruether, *Sexism and God-Talk*, 254.

49. Ruether, *Sexism and God-Talk*, 254-55.

50. Ruether, *Sexism and God-Talk*, 254.

51. Ruether, *Sexism and God-Talk*, 255.

52. Ruether, "Eschatology and Feminism," 139.

53. Ruether, *Sexism and God-Talk*, 256.

54. Suchocki, *God, Christ, Church*, 198.

55. Marjorie Hewitt Suchocki, *The Fall to Violence: Original Sin in Relational Theology* (New York: Continuum, 1995), 153.

56. Suchocki, *The Fall to Violence*, 87.

57. There is a nice parallel with the work of William Lynch on this point. He also carefully describes transcendence as a step to mental health, whereby one sees a particular experience as one among many and is no longer trapped by the "prison of the instant."

58. Wendy Farley, *Tragic Vision and Divine Compassion: A Contemporary Theodicy* (Louisville: Westminster/John Knox Press, 1990), 13.

59. Farley, *Tragic Vision and Divine Compassion*, 13.

60. Farley, *Tragic Vision and Divine Compassion*, 53.

61. Farley, *Tragic Vision and Divine Compassion*, 53.

62. Farley, *Tragic Vision and Divine Compassion*, 13, 23.

63. Farley, *Tragic Vision and Divine Compassion*, 86.

64. Farley, *Tragic Vision and Divine Compassion*, 115.

65. Farley, *Tragic Vision and Divine Compassion*, 127.

66. Farley, *Tragic Vision and Divine Compassion*, 39.

67. Farley, *Tragic Vision and Divine Compassion*, 133.

68. Farley, *Tragic Vision and Divine Compassion*, 133.

69. Kathleen M. Sands, *Escape from Paradise: Evil and Tragedy in Feminist Theology* (Minneapolis: Fortress Press, 1994), 61.

70. Farley, *Tragic Vision and Divine Compassion*, 22.

71. Sands, *Escape from Paradise*, 2.

72. Sands, *Escape from Paradise*, 2.

73. Sands, *Escape from Paradise*, 168.

74. Sands, *Escape from Paradise*, 167.

75. Sands, *Escape from Paradise*, 169.

76. Farley, *Tragic Vision and Divine Compassion*, 130-31.

77. Farley, *Tragic Vision and Divine Compassion*, 119.

78. Farley, *Tragic Vision and Divine Compassion*, 132.

79. Moltmann, *Theology of Hope*, 179.

80. Moltmann, *Theology of Hope*, 179.

81. Moltmann, *Theology of Hope*, 177, 179, 181.

82. Moltmann, *Theology of Hope*, 261.

83. Moltmann, *Theology of Hope*, 119-20.

84. Ellen Ott Marshall, "Practicing Imagination," in *Choosing Peace through Daily Practices*, ed. Ellen Ott Marshall (Cleveland: Pilgrim Press, 2005), 65-85.

Chapter 4: Revisiting Hope's Object and Source

1. See Robert N. Bellah, Richard Madsen, William M. Sullivan, Ann Swidler, and Steven M. Tipton, *Habits of the Heart: Individualism and Commitment in American Life*. First Perennial Library Edition. (New York: Harper & Row, 1985).

2. Sharon Ringe, "Solidarity and Contextuality: Readings of Matthew 18:21-35," in *Reading from This Place: Social Location and Biblical Interpretation*, ed. Fernando Segovia and Mary Ann Tolbert, vol 1 (Minneapolis: Fortress Press, 1994).

3. This distinction between survival and flourishing was made most clear to me during a course with Dr. Victor Anderson, "African American Political Theology." More recently, Womanist literature has deepened my understanding of these values and their interrelatedness. See Rosetta Ross, *Witnessing and Testifying: Black Women, Religion, and Civil Rights* (Minneapolis: Augsburg Fortress Press, 2003), 226-28.

4. Like many Christians, I read such passages from the Hebrew prophets through the lens of Christian eschatology. That is, we read here a description of the *basileia tou theou*. Such a reading involves appropriation, however, and we need to be cognizant of that fact.

5. An extended discussion of these many images is beyond the scope of this text. However, there is a plethora of helpful literature on *basileia* images in the synoptic Gospels. See, for example, G. R. Beasley-Murray, *Jesus and the Kingdom of God* (Grand Rapids: Eerdmans, 1986); Brian K. Blount, *Go Preach! Mark's Kingdom Message and the Black Church Today* (Maryknoll: Orbis, 1998); Bruce Chilton, *Pure Kingdom: Jesus' Vision of God* (Grand Rapids: Eerdmans, 1996); Richard A. Horsley, *Jesus and Empire: The Kingdom of God and the New World Disorder* (Minneapolis: Fortress Press, 2003); Michael L. Humphries, *Christian Origins and the Language of the Kingdom of God* (Carbondale, Ill.: Southern Illinois University Press, 1999); David R. Kaylor, *Jesus the Prophet: His Vision of the Kingdom on Earth* (Louisville: John Knox Press, 1994); Bruce J. Malina, *The Social Gospel of Jesus: The Kingdom of God in Mediterranean Perspective*

(Minneapolis: Fortress Press, 2001); Margaret Anne Moore Robinson, "Moving Beyond Symbol and Myth: Understanding the Kingdom of God through Metaphor" (Ph.D. diss., Claremont Graduate University, 2004); Norman Perrin, *Jesus and the Language of the Kingdom: Symbol and Metaphor in New Testament Interpretation* (Philadelphia: Fortress Press, 1976); Sharon H. Ringe and H. C. Paul Kim, eds., *Literary Encounters with the Reign of God* (New York: T&T Clark International, 2004).

6. Perrin, *Jesus and the Language of the Kingdom: Symbol and Metaphor in New Testament Interpretation*, 30.

7. Moore Robinson, "Moving Beyond Symbol and Myth," 10.

8. Malina, *The Social Gospel of Jesus*, 1.

9. Malina, *The Social Gospel of Jesus*, 1.

10. Horsley, *Jesus and Empire: The Kingdom of God and the New World Disorder*.

11. Malina makes good use of a sociological distinction between low context and high context societies. "Low context societies produce detailed verbal documents that spell out as much as possible, leaving little to the imagination. . . . High context societies produce sketchy and impressionistic documents, leaving much to the reader's or hearer's imagination." The United States is a low context society, but the "'kingdom of God' comes from a high context society and is a high context term" (3). Thus, before applying this high context term to a particular society, one must fill in the details, to understand as much as possible what social, political, and economic details were assumed.

12. Hartt, "Encounter and Inference in Our Awareness of God" in *The God Experience: Essays in Hope*, ed. Joseph P. Whelan, S.J. (New York: Newman Press, 1971), 49.

13. I am indebted to Molly Graver for introducing me to this phrase and its meaning in El Salvador.

14. Paul Tillich, "The Right to Hope: A Sermon," in *Paul Tillich: Theologian of the Boundaries*, ed. Mark Kline Taylor (Minneapolis: Fortress Press, 1991), 330.

15. American Museum of Natural History. Hall of Biodiversity: Spectrum of Life information page available from http://amnh.org/exhibitions/perma nent/biodiversity (accessed April 28, 2006).

16. Tillich, "The Right to Hope: A Sermon."

17. Walter Rauschenbusch, *Christianity and the Social Crisis* (New York: Macmillan, 1907; repr., Louisville: Westminster/John Knox Press, 1991), 94.

18. Luc Jacquet, *March of the Penguins* (Warner Independent, 2005).

19. Isaac Watts, "O God, Our Help in Ages Past," *The United Methodist Hymnal: Book of United Methodist Worship* (Nashville: United Methodist Publishing House, 1989), 117.

20. Sharon Welch, *A Feminist Ethic of Risk* (Minneapolis: Augsburg Fortress, 1989; rev. ed. 2000), 111.

21. Welch, *A Feminist Ethic of Risk*, 111.

22. Anna Case-Winters, *God's Power: Traditional Understandings and Contemporary Challenges* (Louisville: Westminster John Knox, 1990), 208.

23. Wendy Farley, *Tragic Vision and Divine Compassion: A Contemporary Theodicy* (Louisville: Westminster/John Knox Press, 1990), 86.

24. Farley, *Tragic Vision and Divine Compassion*, 86.

25. Farley, *Tragic Vision and Divine Compassion*, 86.

26. Farley, *Tragic Vision and Divine Compassion*, 85, 86.

27. Farley, *Tragic Vision and Divine Compassion*, 87.

28. Farley, *Tragic Vision and Divine Compassion*, 116.

29. Farley, *Tragic Vision and Divine Compassion*, 112.

30. Farley, *Tragic Vision and Divine Compassion*, 88-89.

31. Many who agree on a concept of God's power disagree with me on this point, arguing instead that God could act without human help, but chooses not to. I was reminded of this most recently by a colleague, Dr. Philip Clayton.

32. Case-Winters, *God's Power*, 211.

33. A. Elaine Brown Crawford, *Hope in the Holler: A Womanist Theology* (Louisville: Westminster/John Knox, 2002).

34. Crawford, *Hope in the Holler*, 17 (her italics).

35. Crawford, *Hope in the Holler*, 37.

36. Crawford, *Hope in the Holler*, 27 (my italics).

37. I am reminded of Adolf von Harnack's point about miracles in his text, *What Is Christianity*. "Miracles, it is true, do not happen; but of the marvelous and

the inexplicable there is plenty." Translated by Thomas Bailey Saunders. First Fortress Press Edition (Philadelphia: Fortress, 1986), 28.

38. James W. Fowler, *To See the Kingdom: The Theological Vision of H. Richard Niebuhr* (Nashville: Abingdon, 1974; repr., Eugene, Ore.: Wipf & Stock, 2001), 2.

39. Fowler, *To See the Kingdom*, 5.

40. H. Richard Niebuhr, "Theology in a Time of Disillusionment," in *Theology, History, and Culture* (New Haven: Yale University Press, 1996). What follows is a brief summary of pages 103-109.

41. H. R. Niebuhr, "Theology in a Time of Disillusionment," 103-105.

42. H. R. Niebuhr, "Theology in a Time of Disillusionment," 103.

43. H. R. Niebuhr, "Theology in a Time of Disillusionment," 112.

44. H. R. Niebuhr, "Theology in a Time of Disillusionment," 113.

45. H. Richard Niebuhr, *Radical Monotheism and Western Culture: With Supplementary Essays*, with a foreword by James Gustafson (New York: Harper, 1960; repr., Louisville: Westminster/John Knox, 1993).

46. H. R. Niebuhr, *Radical Monotheism*, 38.

47. H. Richard Niebuhr, *Faith on Earth: An Inquiry into the Structure of Human Faith* (New Haven: Yale University, 1989).

48. H. Richard Niebuhr, *Faith on Earth*, 60.

49. Welch, *A Feminist Ethic of Risk*, 33.

50. Welch, *A Feminist Ethic of Risk*, 33.

51. Barbara Kingsolver, *High Tide: Essays from Now or Never* (New York: HarperCollins, 1995), 15.

Chapter 5: The Practice of Hope

1. Human chorionic gonadotropin is the hormone produced in pregnancy.

2. Paul Tillich, "The Right to Hope: A Sermon," in *Paul Tillich: Theologian of the Boundaries*, ed. Mark Kline Taylor (Minneapolis: Fortress Press, 1991), 327.

3. Mike Taibbi, "Mothers of Deployed Marines Bond Online: Website creates virtual 'band of mothers.'" July 27, 2005. Accessed online http://www. msnbc. msn.com/id/8729098 August 3, 2005.

4. Ellen Knickmeyer and Naseer Nouri, "Stampede in Baghdad Kills over

800 Shiite Pilgrims," Washington Post Foreign Service. Thursday, September 1, 2005; A01. Acccessed on line http://www.washingtonpost.com/wp-dyn/con tent/article/2005/08/31/AR2005083100450_pf.html> September 10, 2005.

5. Sharon Welch, *A Feminist Ethic of Risk* (Minneapolis: Augsburg Fortress, 1989; rev. ed. 2000), 104.

6. Welch, *A Feminist Ethic of Risk*, 14.

7. Welch, *A Feminist Ethic of Risk*, 37.

8. Rebecca Solnit, *Hope in the Dark: Untold Stories, Wild Possibilities* (New York: Nation Books, 2004), 86-87.

9. Barbara Kingsolver, *Small Wonder: Essays* (New York: Perennial Harper Collins, 2002), 4.

10. Solnit, *Hope in the Dark*, 81.

11. Barbara Kingsolver, *High Tide: Essays from Now or Never* (New York: HarperCollins, 1995), 15.

12. William W. How, "For All the Saints," *The United Methodist Hymnal: Book of United Methodist Worship* (Nashville: United Methodist Publishing House, 1989), 711.

Index

Made in the USA
Columbia, SC
16 January 2021

31058306R00087